Praise for

THE OVERLOOKED VOICES OF HURRICANE KATRINA

"In capturing the voices and lived experiences of Black Mississippi middle-class women survivors of Hurricane Katrina, Davis generates two important interventions. She makes the reader aware of and provides important insights into the past experiences and survival strategies of a previously overlooked group of dynamic, resilient women. Yet the book also speaks to the present by providing timely and pertinent lessons for prevention and recovery for Black and minority communities that, due to the legacy of discrimination and environmental injustice, sit in the path of what is expected to be an increasing number of future climate disasters."

BONNIE THORNTON DILL
Professor and Dean, University of Maryland College Park

"Dr. Ophera Davis has given the world a gift that is deeply researched and beautifully written. *The Overlooked Voices of Hurricane Katrina* centralizes and amplifies the voices of Black women in ways that allow for a completely new understanding of how a natural disaster laid bare the inequities of Southern Black life. But Davis doesn't only explore disasters. This transformative research is a story of resilience, care, and recovery. I have no doubt that Davis will inspire the field to seek out marginalized voices. Davis is not merely adding to what we know about the aftermath of Katrina. Because of her careful scholarship, the overlooked are now heard, seen, and, most importantly, valued."

KELLIE CARTER JACKSON
Associate Professor, Wellesley College, Author of *Force and Freedom: Black Abolitionists and the Politics of Violence*

"This groundbreaking book is an amazing collection of firsthand accounts of the hidden stories of Hurricane Katrina Mississippi Black women survivors. If you want to better understand the complexity and diversity of women's experiences with Hurricane Katrina, this is the book to read. Davis captures the voices and lived experiences of these Mississippi women, who discuss how Black women in the South have always dealt with and overcome challenges in life.

"As a Southern Black women researcher, Dr. Davis authentically allows the unheard voices of Mississippi Black women Hurricane Katrina survivors to come to the forefront. She lets these women tell it like it is. These women survivors give readers a glimpse at how Black women have and continue to overcome obstacles and take lemons and make lemonade even when there is very little sugar.

"Lastly, disaster experts can learn a lot from reading this trailblazing book because the insights that Davis uncovers by letting the women tell their own stories will help preparedness, mitigation, and recovery efforts before hurricanes smash ashore. Dr. Davis has a lot to share with a wide range of audiences about how these Mississippi women are resilient and have rebuilt their lives, something Black Southern women have been doing for generations."

RUSSEL L. HONORÉ

LTG, USA, Retired, 33rd Commanding General, US First Army Commander, Joint Task Force, Katrina

The Overlooked Voices of Hurricane Katrina:

The Resilience and Recovery of Mississippi Black Women

By Ophera A. Davis Ph.D.

© Copyright 2021 Ophera A. Davis

ISBN 978-1-64663-429-3

Published by

◤ köehlerbooks ™

3705 Shore Drive
Virginia Beach, VA 23455
800—435—4811
www.koehlerbooks.com

THE OVERLOOKED VOICES OF HURRICANE KATRINA

THE RESILIENCE AND RECOVERY OF

MISSISSIPPI BLACK WOMEN

OPHERA A. DAVIS Ph.D.

VIRGINIA BEACH
CAPE CHARLES

DEDICATION

THIS BOOK IS DEDICATED to my elders. I stand on your shoulders.

To the women in my family: I remember when Mother took me to see my fourth-generation maternal grandmother, Susie, who I saw on several occasions in Mississippi although you were bedridden—what a profound memory I have of you, including your home-going service. Dearest paternal great-grandmother, Catherine, who was also born into slavery. You went to glory before I could see you in person, but the photos of you are amazing, and I thank you for the womanist spirit you passed down the family line that I have heard about from family members over the years.

To the women who experienced Hurricane Katrina, whether grandmothers, mothers, aunts, sisters, nieces, granddaughters, non-binary, or straight whose voices have never been heard, this book is for you. To the women who perished after the storm, let this book make people think of you and the remarkable stories you would have shared. To the women whose stories are still unknown and sidelined, may this work serve as an impetus for researchers to initiate new projects that add their stories to the disaster canon. To the incredible women who gave me the privilege of interviewing you over the years since Hurricane Katrina, I hope this volume is a clear indicator that your experiences and voices will never be silenced again. Thank you for allowing me to tell your stories.

TABLE OF CONTENTS

FOREWORD: 5

CHAPTER 1: INTRODUCTION 11

CHAPTER 2: WHAT HAPPENED IN MISSISSIPPI? 17

CHAPTER 3: IT'S COMING: HURRICANE KATRINA'S APPROACH &
THE WOMEN'S EVACUATION 38

CHAPTER 4: KATRINA WAS TERRIBLE: RETURNING HOME AFTER THE DISASTER. . . .46

CHAPTER 5: EMPLOYMENT AND ECONOMICS—NOW WHAT? 66

CHAPTER 6: THE SUSTAINING FORCE:
SOMETHING WITHIN AND ANGELS FROM GOD .85

CHAPTER 7: AFTER A DECADE:
WHERE ARE THE WOMEN AND HOW ARE THEY DOING? 105

CHAPTER 8: TIME HAS PASSED, LIFE IS BETTER:
CONCLUSION AND RECOMMENDATIONS 121

APPENDIX 126

ACKNOWLEDGMENTS 135

REFERENCES 137

FOREWORD:

"Storm surge, high rivers and rain . . . "[1] When I wrote this, Tropical Storm Barry was gathering momentum on the Gulf Coast of the United States, threatening to become a hurricane, and again placing the people of Louisiana and Mississippi on edge. Whether or not the storm becomes a hurricane, it has already brought flood waters into neighborhoods, homes, and businesses in the Gulf region, and images abound of people wading their way through flooded streets, babies and belongings in hand, seeking safety, fearing danger and destruction. These scenes inspire anxiety—not only in me, 1500 miles away, but more specifically in those who remember Katrina.

Hurricane Katrina was a disaster like no other in United States history. Not only was it tremendous in its meteorological scale and scope, but it was also terrible in its sociological scale and scope. It has become one of America's most iconic disasters. Due in part to the role of the media, it was the first natural disaster on U.S. soil to expose beyond any doubt how natural disasters exacerbate and amplify

---

1   "'Look, there are three ways that Louisiana floods: storm surge, high rivers and rain. We're going to have all three,' Gov. John Bel Edwards said Thursday in a news conference." In Madeline Holcombe and Derek Van Dam, "Barry Is a Triple Threat of Storm Surge, High Rivers and Flooding as It Gets Closer to the Louisiana Coast," CNN, Cable News Network, 12 July 2019, www.cnn.com/2019/07/12/us/ tropical-flooding-friday-wxc-trnd/index.html.

existing racial, class, and gender inequalities. No one could deny or explain away the black and brown faces of people who were left behind to suffer and struggle in the aftermath, or the black and brown bodies that were found during the prolonged recovery efforts. Katrina showed America a new and unforgettable face of its own ugly racism.

Yet there was also a women's story to this disaster—specifically, a Black women's story. While most accounts of women and the storm focused on women's vulnerabilities—the fact that women there, as everywhere, were more likely than men to be poor, elderly, caring for others, or subject to violence—a few accounts focused on women's resilience under these conditions of extreme deprivation and women's creative and heroic caring for others similarly situated.[2] In the face of being left to die, many Black women—individually or collectively—rose up to prove defiantly "no, not us, not this time."

The Katrina episode was just one more instance in which Black women could prove what they have already proven so many times across the history of their time in the Americas: "We specialize in the wholly impossible."[3] This bold assertion by Nannie Helen Burroughs, an early 20th century educator, businesswoman, religious leader, and activist, who has been memorialized in the writings of so many contemporary Black women scholars,[4] could serve as a motto for Black women's indomitable survival genius in the face of every possible kind of threat, from slavery to racism to sexism to economic insecurity to . . . natural (and unnatural) *disasters*.

---

2   For an overview of women's vulnerabilities in the face of Hurricane Katrina, see "Women, Disasters, and Hurricane Katrina," IWPR, Institute for Women's Policy Research, 12 July 2019, www.iwpr.org/publications/women-disasters-and-hurricane-katrina/. For a reflection of Black women's resilience in the face of the storm and its aftermath, see Barbara Ransby, "Katrina, Black Women, and the Deadly Discourse on Black Poverty in America," Du Bois Review: Social Science Research on Race, Cambridge Core, Cambridge University Press, 9 Aug. 2006,www.cambridge.org/core/services/aop-cambridge-core/content/view/S1742058X06060140.

3   Gerda Lerner, ed. *Black Women in White America* (New York: Vintage, 1972), 132.

4   See, for example, Darlene Clark Hine, Wilma King, and Linda Reed, *"We Specialize in the Wholly Impossible": A Reader in Black Women's* History (New York: NYU, 1995).

Another oft-repeated phrase that sums up Black women's genius is "making a way out of no way." This popular African America expression, repeatedly invoked by scholars and nonscholars alike,[5] not only refers to survival genius, but also conveys creative genius—genesis, synthesis—that is, the ability to bear forth that which is new, because it either came from "nowhere" or put previously disparate things together in a novel, coherent, and useful way. Whether in Africa, or the Americas—indeed, whether anywhere in the global African diaspora, past or present—Black women have exhibited both survival genius and creative genius, to the benefit of children, families, communities, and even nations—their own and others'. This is the essence of womanism, and the gift of Black women to the world.[6]

This womanist genius is often most visible during catastrophe. When everything is shaken up and nothing is as yet settled down, those with genius and self-possession step forward to lead and help. Catastrophes showcase the skillsets that are otherwise quietly holding whole worlds together for so many—which is the typical

---

5   See, for example, sources as diverse as Monica A. Coleman's scholarly text, *Making a Way Out of No Way: A Womanist Theology* (Minneapolis: Fortress, 2008), and the National Museum of African American History and Culture's exhibition, *Making a Way Out of No Way*, 13 Nov. 2018, archived at https://nmaahc.si.edu/making-way-out-no-way.

6   In addition to the above-referenced book by Monica A. Coleman, see, for example, Alice Walker, *In Search of Our Mothers' Gardens: Womanist Prose* (New York: Harcourt Brace Jovanovich, 1983), Delores S. Williams, *Sisters in the Wilderness: The Challenge of Womanist God-Talk* (Maryknoll, N.Y.: Orbis, 1993), *A Troubling in My Soul: Womanist Perspectives on Evil and Suffering* (Maryknoll, N.Y.: Orbis, 1993), Clenora Hudson-Weems, *Africana Womanism: Reclaiming Ourselves* (Detroit: Bedford Publishers, 1993), *Africa Wo/Man Palava: The Nigerian Novel by Women* (Chicago: University of Chicago, 1995), Mary E. Modupe Kolawole, *Womanism African Consciousness* (Trenton, N.J.: Africa World Press, 1997), Katie G. Cannon, *Katie's Canon: Womanism and the Soul of the Black Community* (New York: Continuum, 1998), Layli Phillips, ed., *The Womanist Reader* (Routledge, 2006), Layli Maparyan, *The Womanist Idea* (New York: Routledge, 2012), Thema Bryant-Davis and Lillian Comas-D az, *Womanist and Mujerista Psychologies: Voices of Fire, Acts of Courage* (Washington, D.C.: American Psychological Association, 2016), Gary L. Lemons, ed., *Building Womanist Coalitions: Writing and Teaching in the Spirit of Love* (Urbana, Illinois: University of Illinois, 2019), and Layli Maparyan, ed., *Womanism Rising* (Urbana, Illinois: University of Illinois, 2020).

positionality for Black women: behind the scenes, nurturing life, keeping things from falling apart, healing hearts, bodies, and souls, providing material, emotional, intellectual, and spiritual resources—for children, for spouses, for parents and grandparents and in-laws and siblings and cousins, for workplaces, for neighborhoods, and, yes, again, for nations and the world. This unsung daily grind produces salvational genius—the ability to step up during catastrophes and make sure that people survive and, ultimately, thrive again.

This work is not, however, without its costs—physical, emotional, spiritual, material, relational. These Africana womanist geniuses are life-givers, yet life doesn't always restore them—us—equally. An imbalance between giving and receiving creates a kind of suffering that must be dealt with, one way or another. For some, it creates the crucible that yields a kind of transcendence. For others, it results in the gradual—or rapid—loss of vitality, which can manifest as unwellness and even result in that ultimate transition euphemistically characterized as "going from labor to reward." For many, the experience falls somewhere in the middle—or at the intersections—of all of these outcomes.

Hurricane Katrina was a disaster's disaster—environmental, social, financial, political, spiritual—in which Africana women were at the epicenter, as victims, helpers, survivors, and rebuilders. In Ophera Davis's *Overlooked Voices of Hurricane Katrina*, we hear twelve women whose lives were turned upside down by that disaster narrate their experiences—of catastrophe, survival, suffering, recovering, resilience, and genius. It's all there. Through her prowess as an interviewer, social psychologist, and womanist theorist, Davis presents us with a sensitive and illuminating account containing nuances of observation that arise from her shared experience as a Gulf Coast native and her identity as an African American female cultural insider. This book is important to the literature on women and disaster for precisely these reasons—but it is also a gift to the fields of American studies, especially Gulf Coast studies, Africana

Studies, womanist studies, and black women's studies more generally. It is also a useful contribution to psychology, social work, and other helping professions, particularly those that embrace trauma-informed perspectives and recognize the resiliency of those marginalized by mainstream society. Davis's book will also be a good and therapeutic read for those—of any race, gender, or class—who lived through the terrible episode now known by its single name: Katrina.

In sum, Ophera Davis's *Overlooked Voices of Hurricane Katrina* is now part of America's survival and recovery story. It belongs to all of us now. And because of Ophera Davis's consciously womanist scholarship, we are now better equipped to tackle the next disaster—natural or manmade—with justice, empathy, compassion, and visionary pragmatism. As climate change advances, and episodes like Katrina become more and more common—not just in the United States but all over the world—the lessons of this book will become more and more germane to our collective ability to emerge from disaster with dignity and humanity intact.

Layli Maparyan, Ph.D.
Wellesley, Massachusetts, USA

CHAPTER 1
INTRODUCTION

"There is material in her [the Black southern woman] well worth your while, the hope in germ of a staunch, helpful, regenerating woman on which, primarily, rests the foundation stones of our future as a race" (p. 25).

—Anna Julia Cooper. 1892. *A Voice From The South: By a Black Woman From The South.* Xenia, OH: Aldine Printing House.

THIS BOOK DOES TWO THINGS. First, it reveals the untold experiences of an overlooked group of Mississippi Black women Hurricane Katrina survivors before, during, and after the disaster. Secondly, the book describes how these women recovered and have rebuilt their lives since 2005, from a longitudinal study that began two months after the disaster. It is grounded in a Womanist framework and narrative theory. The book expands disaster epistemology on race, gender, and class through rich descriptions and analysis of the never-studied experiences of Mississippi Black women survivors.

This study is unique in that it provides data on a rarely covered stage of disasters, namely recovery and reconstruction (Phillips, 2014; Fothergill, 1998; Oliver-Smith, 1996; Hewitt, 1995; Arnold, 1993) since most disaster studies are "limited to a particular moment" (Fothergill, 1998, p. 12) and give only a "reactionary event-based summation"

(Fothergill, 1998, p. 12). In her book, *Women Confronting Natural Disasters: From Vulnerability to Resilience* (2012), Elaine Enarson, a leading woman disaster scholar, highlighted the unique nature of this study's focus on a group of college-educated Mississippi women. Another unconventional and significant aspect of the book is its grounding in Womanist and narrative theory. The Womanist (Phillips, 2006; Hudson-Weems, 2004; Townes, 1993; Weems, 1993; Omuygemi, 1985; Walker, 1983) orientation provides a cultural context through which the experiences of Black women can be effectively described because it was designed to explain their perspective. Womanism allows the standpoint of these Hurricane Katrina Mississippi Black women (Giddings, 2007; Hill Collins, 2000; Thornton Dill, 2001; Clark Hine, 1995; Gray White, 1985) to emerge before, during, and after the catastrophe from their cultural reference group. Also, it promotes social justice and equitable scholarship opportunities. Akin to Womanism, narrative theory allows these women's experiences to be reported not only by the researcher's analysis, but also through the participants' own voices through extended transcripts of their words (Weissman, 2016; Riessman, 2008; Vaz, 1997) and biographical data (Hunter, 2010; Ransby, 2006; Brown, 1976). It also provides a process through which equitable scholarship can bring the overlooked and marginalized voices from the periphery to the center (hooks, 1984).

In 2005, Hurricane Katrina was the fifth most intense Atlantic basin storm since records began in 1851, and it caused widespread devastation along the eighteen-mile Mississippi Gulf Coastline. After the storm hit, on August 29th, the entire state was declared a disaster area. Mississippi was particularly vulnerable during Katrina because of hurricanes' counterclockwise spin, also known as the dirty side of the storm. This meant that Mississippi bore the brunt of the disaster. Basic necessities, such as electricity and water, were not working for more than a week after the disaster. Katrina's estimated damage in Mississippi was $125 billion (*Science Daily*, 2015), 236 people died, and sixty-seven souls went missing (Johnston, 2018; Walker and Walker, 2015).

The size of Hurricane Katrina in the Gulf of Mexico.

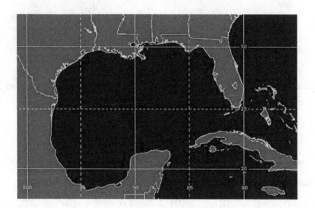

An aerial of the Gulf of Mexico.

Hurricane Katrina's approach to the Mississippi Coastline.

The plight of Mississippi survivors in the years following Katrina remains largely unexamined by most disaster scholars. To remedy that oversight, this book chronicles a group of Mississippi Black women's experiences over a ten-year period. Readers will experience the disaster with the women who lived in three Mississippi cities, Pass Christian, Gulfport, and Biloxi, in two of the state's coastal counties, Hancock and Harrison respectively.

The regional map below shows the location of each of the Mississippi Gulf Coast cities and counties.

This study is based on interviews conducted by the author over a ten-plus-year period with twelve women. All of the women lived on the Mississippi Gulf Coast before the storm and still reside there today. The longitudinal nature of the study offers readers, scholars, and policymakers a rare opportunity to learn about the lived experience of Black women disaster survivors. The design, data management procedure, use of secondary sources for verification purposes, and data analysis process are set out in detail in the Appendix. The theoretical grounding of the study, Womanist framework, and Narrative Theory will be discussed in depth in the next chapter, along with an overview of disaster literature.

In chapter three, the Mississippi woman survivors talk about how they prepared for the storm's arrival and made plans to evacuate. Each woman has been given a pseudonym, to protect her identity, but the city in which she lives is given. The chapter reveals how the women used their social and cultural capital to gather information about the storm, make decisions about what they would do, and decide when and to where they would evacuate before the hurricane washed ashore. These women's behavior and thoughts are analyzed through a Womanist lens, and readers are able to understand their logic, self-awareness, and discipline to show the complexity of their identity. Likewise, the strategies and actions they employed to keep their families safe during the hurricane are discussed.

Chapter four allows the women to tell a part of their evacuation experience through the lens of Narrative Theory. The women's graphic descriptions of the storm's force, as it moved through their Gulf Coast cities, are vivid and moving, unlike any told in disaster scholarship. They speak of the loss of their homes, personal businesses, sections of their neighborhoods, and describe how they began the process of recovery after Hurricane Katrina. Key Womanist tenets are evident in their narratives and are discussed in depth.

Chapter five explores how Hurricane Katrina affected the region's economy—and the economic lives of these Mississippi Black women survivors. The women discuss how they responded to their employment dilemma that was forced upon them after the disaster. An analysis of their narratives reveals how Womanist principles such as self-determination, stamina, and fluidity enabled them to handle their dire circumstances and thrive.

In chapter six, the women discuss the influences that played a prominent role in their ability to refocus after Hurricane Katrina to start rebuilding their lives. The Womanist principle of spirituality permeates their narratives. The women's rich personal accounts show how their faith empowered them to move forward and are rooted in collectivism, another core Womanist principle. Also, their narratives reveal the key role played by volunteers, who arrived by the busloads to lend a hand following the storm, to assist the women's personal recovery and the reconstruction of their communities.

Chapter seven empowers these Mississippi women survivors to discuss where they are ten years after the hurricane. The chapter shows evidence that the women are in the recovery stage and explains how they worked diligently to re-establish the station in life that they were accustomed to prior to the catastrophe. The women's narratives describe what they have accomplished, such as remodeling, rebuilding, or purchasing new homes, finding new jobs, vacationing, and more. In addition, the chapter provides examples of goals the women set and have achieved since Katrina. Some of the women discuss cheerful surprises since the storm that are heartwarming. A Womanist cornerstone, flexibility, is pervasive in this chapter, revealing the women's ability to adjust after Hurricane Katrina. The women's plasticity and self-determination underpinned their Womanist standpoint, which enabled them to use their individual and collective agency, with or without institutional assistance, to do what needed to be done to propel them to a place of normalcy after the disaster. Their narratives are inspirational illustrations of their determination and resilience.

The final chapter explains why this analysis of Mississippi Black women's experiences adds a valuable contribution to the disaster canon. These marginalized and unheard women used their cultural and social capital to access resources for housing, locate jobs, and help their communities as they worked through the process of recovery. Lastly, this chapter offers insight to researchers and policymakers for future studies. It outlines cultural policy considerations that can be instituted to assist people throughout the disaster process to ensure that *every survivor* has agency so that all voices are heard, acknowledged, and responded to before, during, and after hurricanes.

CHAPTER 2
WHAT HAPPENED IN MISSISSIPPI?

HURRICANE KATRINA SLAMMED into the Gulf of Mexico on August 29, 2005. Like most Americans, I watched the horrific images unfolding on television. In the days following the disaster, the coverage focused on what was happening inside and outside the Louisiana Superdome, in New Orleans, where predominantly low-income Black women were sheltering in horrible conditions. While this was very important, there was almost no mention of Mississippi Hurricane Katrina survivors. I knew that if New Orleans was flooded, the Mississippi Gulf Coastline must have been severely damaged because Gulfport, Mississippi, the second largest city in the state, is only about an hour's drive and less than eighty miles from the Crescent City. Since the people in the Superdome were impacted, I knew Mississippians were affected too.

The Mississippi Gulf Coast was a place I had spent summer vacations with family over the years because I grew up in the central part of the state. As a newly minted PhD, now living in Boston, and a lecturer at a number of colleges, I was determined not to sit on the sidelines silently watching. I decided to do what I was trained to do—I would initiate a study on women survivors of Hurricane Katrina. A mentor and colleague at Boston College, Professor David Blustein, told me that his master's student, Marie Land, who is Caucasian and from New Orleans, might be interested in working with me.

Marie and I had several conversations and decided we would use a qualitative approach to conduct the study with women survivors of Hurricane Katrina from New Orleans and Mississippi. Each of us would locate and interview women from our home states. Next, we developed several research questions to ask the women we found to interview. In October 2005, we interviewed African-American and Caucasian women from New Orleans and the Mississippi Gulf Coast. After transcribing our interviews, we met in November to compare transcripts and begin the data analysis process. Our preliminary findings were published in a Harvard journal, and it was one of the first articles that included Mississippi women survivors from Hurricane Katrina. Marie graduated from the Master's Counseling Psychology program and has since earned her PhD from Pennsylvania State University. I decided to continue the study with the Mississippi women I had interviewed on my own. There were several reasons for this.

Firstly, my interviews were only with Mississippi women and, as I reflected on our preliminary data analysis, several comments the women made during the interviews kept resonating with me. One woman said, "Most of the media coverage was only on New Orleans, but Mississippi took the brunt of the storm." Another woman said, "I'm originally from New Orleans, but we were overlooked here in Mississippi."

Secondly, after discussing my reflections and findings with a few other colleagues and getting feedback, I decided these Mississippi women's stories were worth telling and I would continue to investigate their experiences longitudinally. Hearing them say that they were overlooked or forgotten made me realize I had to tell their stories; it was my way to give back as a Black woman PhD from Mississippi. Privately, I did not want the women to feel forgotten by me too.

Thirdly, I received confirmation of the necessity to write the Mississippi women's stories from one of the leading women disaster scholars at a National Women's Studies Conference. After her session, I approached Elaine Enarson and shared the topic of my work with her.

Enarson (2012) affirmed my work on Mississippi women Hurricane Katrina survivors in her book, *Women Confronting Natural Disasters: From Vulnerability to Resilience*, because of its focus on Mississippi women survivors, which added new knowledge on unheard and marginalized female survivors. While not dedicated to the disaster, I experienced uncanny joy when Hurricane Katrina was mentioned more than once in *Becoming* (2018) by Michelle Obama. I understood that the former First Lady knew that Hurricane Katrina impacted many states as she emphasized the tragic plight of New Orleans survivors, probably because of the media's focus in the days after the storm. I knew that Mrs. Obama was committed to social justice, and her reference drew attention to race, social class, and, most importantly, the need to do the right thing for all people after disasters. Her words encouraged me further to make sure these Mississippi Black women's voices were represented in the canon. What's more, the former first lady's comments reminded me of what the late Toni Morrison said about her "own" work and that of other Black writers' ability to center Black people's narratives because they are a part of the village.

Lastly, after a review of the existing literature on disaster scholarship and work specific to Hurricane Katrina, it was evident that—in addition to the media's focus on New Orleans survivors— very few of the books, studies, and articles focused on Mississippi residents' experiences. Additionally, a Soroptimist report (2008) said that "women were [fourteen] times more likely to die than are men" (p. 1) during disasters, which suggested that Black women, who are more vulnerable and marginalized in society, are at a greater risk.

So, for the reasons listed above, in spite of limited resources, no grant funding, and only a supportive—and well-known—sociologist-scholar and mentor, Bonnie Thornton Dill, to encourage me bi-monthly, I continued until this project was completed. I followed the women year-after-year to ensure that my analysis of their lived experiences would expand the body of knowledge and become a part of the Hurricane Katrina disaster survivors' canon.

WHO ARE THESE WOMEN?

Twenty-four Black-American (hereafter, Black) and Caucasian women were initially interviewed in 2005. At some point in the future, I may write about all the women collectively, but because Mississippi Black women's voices are missing from the Hurricane Katrina canon, an analysis of their overlooked experiences is deemed more important to bring their hidden voices front and center. Contact was lost with several women because attempts to reach them went unanswered, and one woman chose to drop out of the study. In 2006, additional women were recommended by the Black women participants and joined the study.

Since 2008, twelve Mississippi Black women have made up the cohort of this longitudinal case study. Most of these women have lived in Mississippi all of their lives in the Gulf Coast counties of Hancock and Harrison. At the start of the study, in 2005, the age range of the women was between thirty-five and sixty. Although the women have aged since their initial interviews, for clarity, when their age is mentioned, only their age at the time of the first interview and their city of residence will be used throughout the book. Pseudonyms were used for confidentiality and to protect the women's identities. More than half of these women are married, and the others are single. Eleven of the women owned their two- to four-bedroom homes before Hurricane Katrina. A quarter of the women were second-time homeowners. All of the women owned vehicles, and several owned more than one car. Ten of the women have college degrees, three of whom had earned master's degrees before the storm. The other two women have at least two years of college experience. Eleven of the women held professional or white-collar jobs prior to Hurricane Katrina. All the women had evacuation plans. In descriptive statistics tradition, the charts provide a visual analysis of these data.

SURVIVORS SAMPLE

WOMEN'S CITY OF RESIDENCE

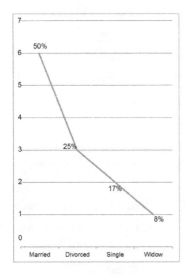

.25

.50

.25

- Gulfport
- Biloxi
- Pass Christian

WOMEN'S AGE RANGE

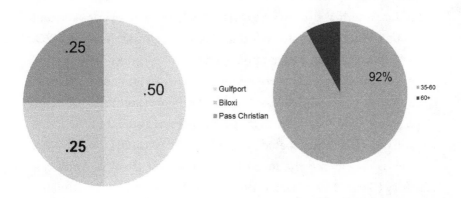

92%

- 35-60
- 60+

WOMEN'S MARITAL STATUS

7	
6	50%
5	
4	
3	25%
2	17%
1	8%
0	
Married Divorced Single Widow	

WOMEN'S PSUEDO NAMES	AGE/2005
LAURA	52
JOANNE	50
BETTY	58
MARY	50
HELEN	45
CORENE	+60
ELLEN	56
LYNNE	50
JEAN	52
SAM	56
CATHERINE	60
JEANETTE	52

LITERATURE REVIEW
Mississippi Disaster History

In Mississippi, four disasters hold historical distinction. Each of these catastrophic events will be discussed to shed light on how the state and her citizenry's experiences have been overlooked and remain obscured from the national disaster narrative. First, in 1863, the *Sultana* sank in Mississippi. To date, the ship's sinking is, still, the worst maritime catastrophe in US history, yet most Americans have never heard of the vessel. The catastrophe occurred 145 years ago and killed more than 1,700 people (Berry, 2005), but the cause is still unknown and debated. Second, the Mississippi Flood of 1927, which is considered the most destructive river flood in American history (Barry, 1998; Daniel, 1977) but is known mostly by students of history and sociology. The Mississippi River broke out of her levee in 145 places, caused more than $400 million in damage, and killed 246 people (Barry, 1998; Daniel, 1977). Thirdly, there is Hurricane Camille, the worst cyclone in Mississippi history until 2005. On August 17, 1969, a Category 5 hurricane made landfall on the Mississippi Gulf Coast. Camille was the only Atlantic hurricane with recorded tidal waves of thirty feet before 1980 (Cutter, 2014; NHC 1969). It is estimated to have had sustained winds of around 190 mph (Cutter, 2014; NHC 1969), but the true wind speed will never be known since the weather equipment was destroyed. One of the worst US hurricanes, Camille, was the worst in Mississippi until Hurricane Katrina.

On Monday morning, August 29, 2005, Hurricane Katrina made her second landfall and nearly washed away the city of Bay St. Louis, Mississippi (NHC, 2005), which was home to about 2,100 residents. Although a Category 3 cyclone when she made landfall, Hurricane Katrina had wind speeds of 125 mph and wind gusts of over 160 mph. Katrina's storm surge was twenty to thirty feet accompanied by ten inches of rain per hour (Cutter, 2014; NHC, 2005). Historian Doug Brinkley (2006) said in *The Great Deluge: Hurricane Katrina,*

New Orleans, and the Mississippi Gulf Coast, "the Mississippi Gulf Coast was getting hammered even harder than Louisiana" (p.148).

Estimates of the financial cost of Hurricane Katrina to Mississippi vary depending on the source. They range from as low as $80 million (Kenyon International, 2006) to $161 billion (Unger, David J. and Noble Ingram, 2018). While these figures are astronomical, they do not capture or include the comprehensive damage to the region or the toll and cost suffered by the disaster's survivors.

After most catastrophes, women's death rates are typically higher than men's (Soroptimist, 2008; Wilson et al., 1996; Begum, 1993), but this was not the case after Katrina in Mississippi. Remarkably, only 236 (Walker and Walker, 2015; Johnston, 2008) Mississippians lost their lives after the catastrophe. The Katrina memorial in Biloxi lists the names of fewer than fifty women who died due to the hurricane (Biloxi, Mississippi, 2016). Before the disaster, women made up over fifty percent of the Mississippi Gulf Coast's population of 400,000 people (US Census, 2005). The ability of the women in this study to keep themselves and their families safe and the death rate low after the natural disaster is—beyond question—astounding. The next section will provide a review of the disaster literature with emphasis on women and race.

GENDER, RACE, AND CLASS IN US DISASTER HISTORY

The first recorded US disaster studies date back to the early twentieth century. Although women were not the focus of the early studies (Struening, 1979; Erickson, 1976; Logue, Holger, and Merton, 1976; Mileti, Drabek, and Haas, 1975; Barton, 1969; Drabek and Boggs, 1968; Moore and Friedsam, 1959; Fritz, 1954; Prince, 1920), a few of them mention women. One citation not included in the list above but is relevant to this book and worth mentioning. In 1944, Ann Petry, a Connecticut resident and Black American woman novelist, provided a first-hand account of her survival of the Great New England Hurricane in her book *Country Place.* Throughout the volume, Petry gives vivid descriptions of many aspects of the hurricane through her characters by detailing residents' preparation for the storm, endurance of the persistent violent force of the shrieking wind, intense beating rain, and the sound of trees crashing to the ground. Also, Petry described the damage to the infrastructure of the town, such as the loss of power and telephone communication for days, damage to the neighborhood roads, churches, and homes, the massive amount of debris as well as the interruption of life, while noting that the day after the storm was a beautiful, crystal-clear day that left people with a surreal, thankful feeling of survival. What's more, Petry's daughter, Elisabeth, discusses and corroborates the impact of the hurricane on her mother, in *At Home Inside: A Daughter's Tribute to Ann Petry* (2009).

Regarding disaster studies, Drabek (1968) found that women were more likely to get prepared than men and evacuate before storms. Likewise, Wilkerson and Perry (1970) found that before Hurricane Camille hit Mississippi in 1969, many women evacuated. The 1980s brought about the first effort to bring the voices of minorities into the disaster canon. Perry and Mushkatel's (1986) book, *Minority Citizens in Disasters* did not focus on women, but highlighted Blacks and Latinos preparedness for catastrophes and their choice to heed evacuation requirements. Another study found that women sought information to protect their homes and families (Miller, Turner, and Kimball, 1981) before disasters more readily than men did (Turner, et al., 1986; Leik, 1982). Two international studies are worth mentioning. Caribbean public health consultant Gloria Noel (1998) noted that women in the West Indies faced more challenges during disasters than did men. European scholar Christine Clason (1983) found that women handled disasters well because they were flexible and adaptable.

During the 1980s, the male-dominated disaster field began to acknowledge the importance of conducting in-depth qualitative studies to understand women's experiences during disasters (Enarson and Morrow, 1998; Phillips, 1997; Scanlon; 1997; Neilsen, 1984). The 1990s ushered in several women disaster scholars (Morrow and Phillips, 1999; Enarson and Morrow, 1998; Fothergill, 1998), and the female voice became a part of the canon. In 1998, the seminal book, *The Gendered Terrain of Disasters: Through Women's Eyes* was published and edited by Elaine Enarson and Betty Morrow. It is a text-reader exclusively focused on women's experiences during and after disasters primarily in the United States. Many findings from the book are noteworthy, and Enarson and Hearn (1998) said that more ethnographies and longitudinal qualitative studies with women disaster survivors were needed. One article in the text by Alice Fothergill (1998) revealed that women's caregiving roles led them to put their families' needs before their own needs. Another finding was more noteworthy from Fothergill's (1998) review of the US disaster women's literature where she stated that "it is impossible to discern, for example, the experience of a black woman" (p. 13). Despite Fothergill's forthright statement, disaster researchers reported that Blacks were less prepared (Tierney, 1989), experienced delayed post-traumatic stress disorder (Green, 1993), had emotional injuries (Shoaf and Harvinder, 1998), and viewed churches and the Red Cross as helpful during recovery (McDonnell et al., 1995). Lastly, Bready and Bolin (1998) said that Blacks' concerns were only represented by the Black media during and after disasters. The next section will discuss research on Hurricane Katrina race and women, followed by a section on Mississippi Hurricane Katrina survivors.

HURRICANE KATRINA AND RACE

This section will discuss books on Hurricane Katrina, race, and umbrella texts primarily about New Orleans survivors. There are a number of social phenomena single-authored books associated with Hurricane Katrina. They include *The Great Deluge: Hurricane Katrina, New Orleans, and the Mississippi Gulf Coast* by Douglas Brinkley (2006) and *Come Hell or High Water: Hurricane Katrina and the Color of a Disaster* by Michael Eric Dyson (2006). A few of the first text-readers include *The Sky is Crying: Race, Class, and Natural Disasters* by Cheryl Kirk-Duggan (2006); *There is No Such Thing as a Natural Disaster: Race, Class, and Katrina* by Gregory Squires and Chester Hartman (2006); and *Unnatural Disaster: The Nation on Hurricane Katrina* by Betsy Reed (2006).

More text-readers were published a few years after the disaster. They include *The Sociology of Katrina: Perspectives on a Modern Catastrophe* by David Brunsma, David Overfelt, and Steven Picou (2007); David Dante Troutt's *After the Storm: Black Intellectuals Explore the Meaning of Hurricane Katrina* (2007); and *The Hurricane Katrina Crisis, Race, and Public Policy Reader* (Manning and Clarke, 2007). Over the years, the number of text readers continues to grow, such as Jeanne Haubert and Elizabeth Fussell's *Rethinking Disaster Recovery: A Hurricane Katrina Retrospective* (2015); *The State, Civil Society, and Displaced Survivors of Hurricane Katrina* by Ronald Angel, Holly Bell, Julie Beausoleil, and Laura Lein (2012); *Displaced: Life in the Katrina Diaspora* by Lynn Weber and Lori Peek (2012); *Resilience and Opportunity: Lessons from the US Gulf Coast after Katrina and Rita* by Amy Liu, Roland Anglin, Richard Mizelle, and Allison Peyer (2011); *Katrina's Imprint: Race and Vulnerability in America* by Keith Wailoo, Karen O'Neill, Jeffrey Dowd, and Roland Anglin (2010); *Race, Place, and Environmental Justice After Hurricane Katrina: Struggles to Reclaim, Rebuild, and Revitalize New Orleans and the Gulf Coast* by Robert Bullard and Beverly Wright (2009); *Overcoming Katrina: African-American Voices from the Crescent City and Beyond* by D'Ann Penner and Keith C. Ferdinand (2009); *Truth Crushed to Earth Will Rise Again: Katrina and Its Aftermath* by Jeremy I. Levitt and Matthew C. Whitaker (2009); and *Voices Rising: Stories From the Katrina Narrative Project* by Rebecca Antoine (2008). It is important to note that although some of these books include language such as, ". . . and the Mississippi Gulf Coast," "and the Gulf Coast," "in America and beyond," there is only a cursory mention of Mississippi survivors in no more than one chapter in each book. Some of the texts mention race and class, but the majority focus on low-income Black survivors from Louisiana.

Finally, three dissertations focus on New Orleans survivors and are relevant. First, Farrah Gafford's work is one of two studies on middle-class survivors from New Orleans. In *Life in the Park: Community Solidarity, Culture, and the Case of a Black Middle-class Neighborhood* (2010), Gafford explores how a group came together after Hurricane Katrina to rebuild a New Orleans community park. Second, a work by Tiffany Williams Bates (2014) offers the New Orleans Black woman's perspective on surviving Hurricane Katrina through the lens of resilience. Bates' (2014) study, *The Survival Experiences of Black Women in New Orleans During and After Hurricane Katrina*, parallels other works on low-income Black women but adds a dimension by showing that some women have flourished. Lastly, Emmanuel David's (2009) study, *Women of the Storm: An Ethnography of Gender, Culture, and Social Movements following Hurricane Katrina*, focuses on a group of predominantly Caucasian women in New Orleans, who are in the middle and upper socioeconomic classes. The group became social activists after the storm. The next section includes works focused specifically on women and Hurricane Katrina.

HURRICANE KATRINA AND WOMEN

Since Hurricane Katrina, the number of studies on Black women has increased. This section will highlight the large number of journal articles and books specifically on black women and Katrina, primarily from New Orleans. Emmanuel David's (2017) book, *Women of the Storm: Civic Activism After Hurricane Katrina*, is described above. Another text, *Surviving Katrina: The Experiences of Low-Income African American Women* by Jessica Pardee (2014), is based on New Orleans survivors. The third book, *The Women of Katrina: How Gender, Race, and Class Matter in an American Disaster* (2012), is a text-reader edited by Emmanuel David and Elaine Enarson. Most of the articles in the volume are focused on low-income Black women from New Orleans, although it includes two papers on Mississippi women. A few books by women disaster scholars discuss several catastrophes and highlight aspects of Hurricane Katrina. They include *Women and Disasters: From Theory to Practice* by Brenda Phillips and Betty Morrow (2008) and *Women Confronting Natural Disasters: From Vulnerability to Resilience* by Elaine Enarson (2012). There are no texts dedicated exclusively to a group of Hurricane Katrina Mississippi Black women survivors' longitudinal experience except this volume.

There are a plethora of journal articles on women and Katrina. However, as mentioned, most are focused on low-income Black women from New Orleans. The papers address issues such as domestic violence (Anastario, Shehab, and Lawry, 2009), battering (Phillips, Jenkins, and Enarson, 2008), death (Sharkley, 2007), displacement (Laditka, Murray, and Laditka, 2010; Litt, 2006; Weber, 2012), single mothers (Tobin-Gurley, 2008), preparedness (Spence, Lachlan, and Griffin, 2007), media representation (Calloway, 2009), survivors who have returned to New Orleans (Tyler, 2007), group formation (David, 2009; Litt, 2006), public housing (DeWeever, 2008), social vulnerability and mental health (Rhodes, Chan, Paxson, Rouse, Waters, and Fussell, 2010; Jenick, 2010), and social inequality (Reid, 2011). Likewise, several reports from The Institute for Women's Policy Research (IWPR) have been released, but one of the first was led by Avis DeWeever, et al. (IWPR, 2005). The report highlights regional statistics on Hurricane Katrina but provides limited data on women survivors from Mississippi. Most of these studies focus on the frenzied aftermath and initial response stage after catastrophes. A few of the studies mentioned above focus on the middle stage of disaster, but none analyze Hurricane Katrina survivors' experiences over time. This book fills several gaps in the literature, due to its focus on Mississippi women survivors and its longitudinal approach by adding an overlooked group of Black women's narratives of recovery after Hurricane Katrina to the official record.

HURRICANE KATRINA: BOOKS ON MISSISSIPPI SURVIVORS

The gap is vast on knowledge of Hurricane Katrina's impact in Mississippi and her citizenry, and disaster scholarship is scant. As mentioned, a number of books include Mississippi in the title, but most give only a cursory mention of Katrina survivors in the state. Only twelve books begin to shed light on Hurricane Katrina's effect on Mississippi and her survivors' experiences. Melody Golding and Sally Pfister created a pictorial tribute, *Katrina: Mississippi Women Remember* (2007), which displayed photos of female survivors from the state. The books of Natasha Trethewey and Jesmyn Ward, two former Mississippi Black fiction writers, are noteworthy. Tretheway mixes personal stories with memories of families' and friends' experiences in *Beyond Katrina: A Meditation on the Mississippi Gulf Coast* (2010). In *Salvage the Bones* (2012), Ward provides a glimpse into Hurricane Katrina's impact on a Mississippi coastal town and one family's experience. Another former Mississippian, Kathleen Koch, takes a similar approach in *Rising from Katrina: How My Mississippi Hometown Lost It All and Found What Mattered* (2010). Seven books offer insight into Hurricane Katrina's impact on Mississippi survivors. They include Jennifer Trivedi's (2020) *Mississippi After Katrina: Disaster Recovery and Reconstruction on the Gulf Coast* which discusses the city of Biloxi and several group experiences pre and post Katrina; former Mississippi governor Haley Barbour's *America's Great Storm: Leading through Hurricane Katrina* (2015); *Katrina Mississippi Voices from Ground Zero* by Nancy Kay Sullivan (2015); Susan Cutter's et. al., *Hurricane Katrina and the Forgotten Coast of Mississippi* (2014); *Hurricane Katrina: The Mississippi Story* by James P. Smith (2012); Ellis Anderson's *Under Surge Under Siege: The Odyssey of Bay St. Louis and Katrina* (2010); and *Post-Katrina Recovery of the Housing Market Along the Mississippi Gulf Coast* by Kevin McCarthy and Mark Hanson (2007). Each text touches upon personal stories of Mississippi men and women, but they are neither longitudinal studies nor are they focused on one group of women. The novelty and significance of this study is that it closely follows one group of Mississippi women over a ten-year period of time before, during, and after Hurricane Katrina and analyzes their experiences of resilience and recovery— something no other study has done.

THEORETICAL FOUNDATION: NARRATIVE THEORY AND WOMANIST FRAMEWORK

Narrative Theory

Narrative theory analysis is the first methodology that frames this longitudinal case study of Mississippi Black women survivors of Hurricane Katrina. In his book, *Aristotle's Poetics*, Jason Mittell (2017) said the roots of narrative theory can be traced back to ancient Sumer. This perspective is buoyed by a growing number of scholars (Asante, 2018; Hagan, Johnston, Monkhouse, and Piquette, 2011; Guisepi, 2003). In the 1900s, narrative theory was used and popularized by the University of Chicago school of sociology, and since then, it has been accepted as a leading interpretive tool by social scientists. Narrative theory (Barusch, 2012) is akin to a qualitative approach (Conyers, 2016) in that it adheres to grounded theory principles (Corbin & Strauss, 2008; Glaser & Strauss, 2000). Several definitions are provided below:

Narrative Theory provides a way to communicate and chronicle a group's experience by revealing personal and cultural information in a coherent sequence (Hall & Powell, 2011).

Renowned Narrative Theory scholar, Catherine Riessman (2008), defines it as talk about events that are consequential and have meaning for the teller and listener. Further, Riessman (2008) says, Narrative Theory provides a way to conduct case-centered research that links events and ideas about participants in meaningful patterns or themes from random disconnectedness.

Gary Weissman (2016) defines narrative theory as a way to evaluate participants' lived experiences by using their own words historically, socially, and culturally.

Sally Hunter (2010) says of Narrative Theory that it enables researchers to use biographical data and large units of text to convey participants' accounts.

Jason Mittell (2017) describes narrative theory as a human science that allows the accounts of participant data to be interpreted by researchers from field interviews which ultimately reveal the accounts of a group's experiences.

Why Narrative Theory?

The definitions above express the ways in which this volume uses narrative theory to describe and analyze the experiences of these Black women Hurricane Katrina survivors. First, it enabled the themes that emerged during the data analysis to be expressed in extensive quotes. Disaster scholar Brenda Phillips (2014) says, "theoretical memos" (p. 119) like narratives enable the researcher to describe each woman's account in depth. Historian Barbara Ransby (2006) poignantly stated that Hurricane Katrina survivors' lived experiences could best be accounted for through narratives or "oral histories" (p. 216). Also, narrative theory allows researchers to use large units of text or biographical data (Rice and Ezzy, 1999) to generate findings from the participants' experiences. The use of lengthy interview transcripts is important and different from traditional quantitative research that usually relies on short quotes that the researcher interprets as the point of view of participants but rarely includes cultural context. In contrast, narrative theory gives participants agency by using lengthy units of data or group quotes to draw out themes and explanations, rather than chance interpretations or inferences about what the data says. This book reveals the major themes found in that analysis.

Second, narrative theory recognizes and authenticates the use of emic perspective (Riessman, 2008; Kottak, 2006) when conducting field research on a social group. In fact, narrative theory enables researchers, specifically those with insider perspective, to observe and give meaning to the ways in which local people think and participate (Barusch, 2012) in the evaluation. What's more, narrative theory deconstructs and reveals participants' personal presuppositions or rationale (Grbich, 1999), and it looks for sociocultural meaning (Lupton, 1999) to build and strengthen the themes that emerge from their experiences. My own sociocultural perspective, as a Black American former Mississippian, with knowledge of the region and the nuances of its cultural mores, helped build trust with the participants and added authenticity to my analysis of their stories. The women had little resistance during the interview process sharing intimate details about their experiences. This "insider perspective" (Ager and Loughry, 2004; Kottak, 2006) is rooted in the participants' belief that the researcher perceives the world and gives meaning to events and circumstances in the same way that they do (Kottak, 2006). Moreover, renowned sociologist, Patricia Hill Collins (2000) posits that Black women intellectuals are best placed to clarify and interpret the standpoint of Black women through their own experience, as situated knowers of sociocultural context.

Third, narrative theory has a unique ability to give voice (Vaz, 1997) to hidden Mississippi Black women. It promotes a Foucauldian-style (Bryne-Armstrong, 2001) of social justice (Hines-Datiri 2017; Bullard and Wright, 2009; Antoine, 2008) by enabling the researcher to purposefully report participants' personal perspectives from case studies as a decisive tool of agency (Vaz, 1997). Also, according to Mittel (2017), narrative theory can be used as a process of interpreting texts or transcripts on participants' sequences of action. This fosters individual respect for participants' intentions, experiences, and histories, which permits researchers to argue their perspectives thematically and meaningfully and assert authenticity of the women survivors' accounts. The methodology's genteel nature enables a different voice (Gilligan, 1985) to emerge as opposed to that of one with a generalist orientation. This allows the author's insider perspective voice to equitably, inclusively, and evenhandedly emerge (Bakhtin, 1981 as cited in Barusch, 2012) as the interpreter of these never-studied Mississippi Black women survivors' experiences so deserves. An example of this process is best seen in the recent publication of the eighty-plus-year-old volume *Barracoon* by renowned Black woman writer, Zora Neale Hurston (2018). Hurston used narrative theory, considered during her time an unconventional methodology to capture the lived experience of her unique interviewee—Cudjo—the last known emancipated living slave in the United States. Hurston's important interview and book yield unknown information, and it provides an excellent narrative theory example for scholars to replicate. Although a century later, like that work, this study follows Hurston's tradition and brings the voices of a hidden group of Mississippi Black women survivors of Hurricane Katrina from obscurity to front and center.

Lastly, narrative theory allows researchers to illustrate through extensive expressions that Hurricane Katrina impacted more than one location or one group before, during, and after the catastrophe. Put another way, narrative theory sanctions the inclusion of vulnerable voices, such as these Mississippi women, by giving them the social and political nod of approval to express themselves in the way that they feel comfortable so that their accounts can become a part of the official Hurricane Katrina archive.

Womanist Framework

The second lens through which these Mississippi Black women survivors' lived experiences is framed and analyzed is Womanism (Phillips, 2006; Weems, 1994; Ogunyemi, 1985; Walker, 1983;). Several foundational definitions are below:

Womanism: 1. From the Black folk expression of mothers to female children, "you acting womanish". Usually referring to audacious, courageous or *willful* behavior, responsible, in charge, *serious*. 2. A woman who loves, appreciates, and prefers women's culture, women's emotional flexibility (values tears as natural counterbalance of laughter), and women's strength. Committed to survival and wholeness of entire people, male *and* female. Not a separatist, except periodically, for health. Traditionally a universalist, as in: "Mama, why are we brown, pink, and yellow, and our cousins are white, beige, and Black?" Ans. "Well, you know the colored race is just like a flower garden, with every color flower represented." Traditionally capable, as in: "Mama, I'm walking to Canada and I'm taking you and a bunch of other slaves with me." Reply: "It wouldn't be the first time." 3. *Loves* the Folk. Loves herself. *Regardless.* 4. Womanist is to feminist as purple is to lavender (Walker, 1983).

Womanism: Characteristics—self-naming and self-defining, family-centered and compatible, flexible with her roles and ambitions, demanding of respect and strong, reverent of elders and authentic, nurturing and mothering (Weems, 1994).

Womanism: The basic tenets of Womanism include a strong self-authored spirit of activism, the role that spirituality and ethics has on ending the interlocking oppression of race, gender, and class that circumscribes the lives of African-American women (Williams, 2013; Phillips, 2006; Gilkes, 2001; Cannon, 1996; Townes, 1993).

As is common in qualitative research, these Mississippi Hurricane Katrina Black women survivors' analyzed narratives were examined through key Womanist concepts. From this process, several Womanist themes were found to be meaningful and purposeful. Each major theme will be described below and later discussed in depth in each chapter as they relate to the women's resilience and recovery. Walker's (1979) first mention of "Womanish," referred to today as Womanist orientation, was a term she said is "strongly rooted in the Black women's culture." According to Walker (1983), researchers can contextualize the implicit expression of the common Black American woman's cultural experience to Womanism just as the term feminist needs no explanation in its reference to Caucasian women. Similarly, other Womanist scholars (Phillips, 2006; Weems, 1993; Ogunyemi, 1985) describe the concept's unique ability to express and permeate Black women's cultural experience. Womanism provides a standpoint through which Black women's sidelined status and personal experiences in American society can be viewed and brought from the margins to the center (hooks, 1984), particularly after events like Hurricane Katrina. Moreover, Womanism provides a platform of self-advocacy (Giddings, 2007; Hines, King, and Reed, 1995; Weems, 1994; Walker, 1983) that compliments the social justice perspective (Bryne-Armstrong, 2001) described in narrative theory and is part and parcel of the framework that propelled these Mississippi Black women survivors of Hurricane Katrina to resiliency and recovery.

There are several tenets of Womanist's orientation that enable Black women to negotiate situations, such as the chaotic aftermath of Hurricane Katrina, and other types of oppression and marginalization, while remaining centered so that they can efficiently move beyond their quandaries. The first characteristic of Womanism found in this study was fluidity. There are many examples throughout the book of the women's openness and ability to remain flexible, and to adjust to unexpected circumstances, in the months and years that followed the hurricane. Also, the women's plasticity underpins the strength they found to endure and recover after the catastrophe.

A second Womanist characteristic demonstrated by these women was their universalist or collectivist outlook. The women did not feel responsible only for their individual and familial survival, but they were concerned about and desired to assist and uplift the group. There are many examples of this disposition in action immediately after the storm. Patricia Hill Collins calls a Black woman's act of serving as the other mother[s] (2000) their way of showing care and concern for members of their cultural group. Carol Stack's (1975) book, *All Our Kin: Strategies for Survival in a Black Community*, showed that Black women will work tirelessly for the preservation of their families and communities. This trait was observed in these Mississippi women after Katrina and is evident in several chapters. Moreover, these women's accountability for themselves, their families, communities, and all groups speak to the pro-human stance of Womanism.

Still another Womanist's precept displayed was a spirit of activism (Phillips, 2006), which includes self-willed resourcefulness and the initiation of new projects and completion of goals in spite of crushing dilemmas—in this case, dealing with the aftermath of Katrina. Several women's narratives reveal how they became change agents in their communities by sharing information or speaking up for the group members to make sure that their needs were met. These Womanist characteristics have been an intrinsic part of Black women's nature before the times of Sojourner Truth and Harriet Tubman.

Faith is another key tenet of Womanism (Williams, 2013; Phillips, 2006; Gilkes, 2001; Townes, 1993). Almost all of these Mississippi women survivors spoke of the importance of spirituality in their lives. Womanism's theological orientation (Williams, 2013; Phillips, 2006; Gilkes, 2001; Cannon, 1996; Townes, 1994) was, arguably, central to the post-Katrina recovery of more than three quarters of the women in the study. Patricia Hill Collins (1998) broadened the principle when she noted that "spirituality is not merely a system of religious belief similar to logical systems of ideas. . . " but rather, ". . . spirituality comprises articles of faith that provide a conceptual framework for living everyday life" (p. 11). This is how these Mississippi Black women describe its impact on their recovery. Put another way, this Womanist holistic principle served as one of the integral components of their consciousness (Phillips, 2012) and a guiding principle of their philosophy of life, or *sine qua non*, that ultimately led to their universalist actions and plasticity. The cultural norms of religious affiliation and the co-opting of faith traditions have been a practice of women from the African diaspora, since the times of the female Pharaoh Hatshepsut.

Lastly, although only the overarching Womanist themes were discussed above, almost all of its principles were observed and will be evident in the women's narratives. The experiences of these obscured Mississippi women survivors, whose voices have not been heard, are worth telling and need to be understood through an orientation that inherently and authentically represents their perspective. Womanism explains how these Mississippi women's experiences shaped their actions before, during, and after Hurricane Katrina because it was created to describe Black women's orientation.

CHAPTER 3
IT'S COMING:
HURRICANE KATRINA'S APPROACH &
THE WOMEN'S EVACUATION

KATRINA WAS THE FIFTH HURRICANE of the 2005 season. She formed in the middle of August and was initially predicted to turn back toward the Atlantic Ocean, but on August 24th, she turned westward and entered the Gulf of Mexico. The warm sea water on the Gulf Coast caused Katrina to intensify to a Category 3 hurricane, and within twenty-four hours, the cyclone was upgraded to a Category 4 storm. A day before the storm came ashore, it rapidly increased in strength to become a Category 5 hurricane. Due to the storm's change in direction and magnification, forecasters' warnings shifted dramatically, with grave concern for Gulf Coast residents.

In disaster scholarship, warning confirmation (Draber and Stephenson, 1971) is the information one has about an approaching storm. The Mississippi Black women survivors in this study prepared for the storm as well as they could. Hurricane Katrina approached the Gulf of Mexico (hereafter, referred to as the Mississippi Gulf Coast, Gulf Coast, or the Coast, as the women describe their neighborhoods) during the final days of August 2015. Hurricane season runs from June 1st to November 30th annually, so the women were familiar with the process. Some of these Mississippi women talked to family members, while others coordinated, secured, and boarded up their homes. In addition, they found places to evacuate, for themselves and their families, before the storm's arrival. All of these Katrina women survivors planned to evacuate. This chapter empowers the women to describe their actions and explain their experiences in the narrative tradition using Womanist tenets, in their own words.

The narratives will highlight some of the women's decision to leave as early as a week before the storm arrived. Other women describe their harrowing experience of evacuating days before the hurricane in heavy traffic. The core tenets of Womanism are evident as the women discuss how they protected themselves and their property before the hurricane. Also, the women's narratives point to their spirituality, ability to make and adjust their plans, and remain flexible as the hurricane approached the Mississippi Gulf Coast. But, in spite of their evacuation plans, two of the women had to wait the storm out because of concern and care for family members. Before hearing the experiences of the evacuees, the women who stayed behind will discuss the dilemma in which they found themselves before the hurricane washed ashore.

Laura, Gulfport, Mississippi

I was waiting for my son, who was working. You see, he worked for the city of Gulfport, and they were busy securing all of the city's properties. Although he had his own apartment, we had decided that webwould evacuate together after he got off work. So, while I waited for him to get off work, I was busy getting the outdoor furniture put in one of the storage houses behind my house with the help of friends and a neighbor. We had boarded up the windows on my house yesterday. My plan was to evacuate to Jackson [Mississippi] when my son got here, but by the time he got here, it was too late. The weather was too intense to leave, so we had to stay here at my house [she lived in a three-bedroom ranch-style home] until the storm passed.

Another woman, Betty, who lived in Gulfport did not evacuate because her father, who was eighty years of age, refused to leave the family home that he had built thirty-five years earlier.

Betty, Gulfport, Mississippi

My father said, "I built this house with five inches of Stucco on it and it's up on a hill. It survived every storm since [19]45. It survived [Hurricane] Camille and other storms, so I am not going anywhere." After my dad said that, I knew I was going to have to stay there with him, because I am his primary caregiver. So I started calling my brothers and sisters and convinced them that they had to get their children and leave as soon as possible because the storm was headed to the Gulf Coast. All of them evacuated to Jackson, Mississippi, so that they would be safe. My husband now (though we were not married at the time) stayed with me and my dad to wait out the storm. [Betty made this statement several times during the interview. It was clear to me that she wanted to be transparent and authentic.]

As the other Mississippi women in this study were aware of, or watched, local weather forecasters projecting the path of the storm, they began to put their evacuation plans into action. Some of them left almost a week before the hurricane hit, and others left as late as one day before Katrina moved inland. Now they describe their evacuation experiences.

Ellen, Biloxi, Mississippi

After living on the Gulf Coast over twenty years, I knew the routine well. Over the years, my husband and I have boarded up several homes on the Coast, and we have always evacuated when there was a threat of a Category 3 or higher hurricane in the region. Since my hometown is in Booneville [the northern part of Mississippi, which was about three hundred miles from Biloxi], we always just go home for a visit with family until the storm passes. I talked to my sister in Booneville on the weekend before Katrina hit, and we talked about the storm's projected path. I told her we were coming home since this storm might be bad and may be headed toward the Gulf [of Mexico]. So after we got the house boarded up, got the insurance papers, and a few other valuables, in a suitcase, my husband and I evacuated on the Tuesday before Katrina hit [six days before the storm's arrival]. We drove to Booneville [on Tuesday, August 23, 2005]. We planned to return a few days after the storm had passed as we always had.

Helen, Gulfport, Mississippi
I grew up in Monticello, Mississippi [the northeastern part of the state, about 260 miles from the Gulf Coast], and most of my family still lives there. After talking to my sister, I decided I would leave, but I needed to finish getting my house boarded up. [Helen owned a three-bedroom home. As the storm approached, Helen said,] I talked to several friends, you know, we helped each other board up our homes when hurricanes threatened and when the weatherman says they [hurricanes] are headed to the Coast [Gulf of Mexico or Mississippi Gulf Coast]. After coordinating things and securing our home, I packed a suitcase, got in my SUV, and drove to Monticello on the Thursday [August 25th, four days before Katrina hit]. See, I am afraid of hurricanes since I didn't grow up on the Coast.

Jean, Biloxi, Mississippi

. . . by the time Katrina hit, I had evacuated to Houston. I convinced my grown kids to evacuate and come where I was until the storm was over.

Jeanette, Pass Christian, Mississippi

I evacuated with my husband on Saturday, 27 August [two days before Hurricane Katrina]. We were watching CNN and the Weather Channel during the preceding week before Katrina hit, [and] we started looking at our options. We started making plans to evacuate. I was able to make reservations and got one of the last rooms that was available at a hotel in Hattiesburg [about forty-five miles north of the Mississippi Gulf Coast] from Saturday to Monday. At first, we were going to leave on Friday, but we decided to leave Saturday morning. After getting the house boarded up, we packed water, clothes, made sure we had all the necessary provisions, like laptops, cell phones, chargers, checkbooks, credit cards, etc. Then, before we got ready to lock the door, I asked my husband if he had the insurance papers. I just felt like it was going to be bad, call it an internal feeling, intuition or whatever, I just thought this is going to be bad. As we left the Coast, we talked to family to let them know where we would be. I called my mother who had evacuated with my sister a few days before from Louisiana to let them know where we were going. We talked to my cousin who lives in Alexandria, Virginia, so that he would know where we were. We got to Hattiesburg by mid-morning, and we were sure we were out of harm's way. We planned to go back to the Coast after the storm passed.

Sam, Pass Christian, Mississippi

I've seen storms come and go. Because I was considered

essential personnel on my job, I had to work until Saturday to shut down the company. Katrina was a threat to the region, but she changed course so rapidly and came directly into our area. While I was at work, my two grown sons boarded up their homes and my house. Since the traffic was backed up, we thought it was too late to evacuate to Alabama, which was what we normally did, so we decided to go to church that Sunday morning. Then, my sons, daughter-in-law, niece, and I evacuated to a cousin's house, inland, in Kiln, Mississippi [twenty-six miles inland]. She opened her 8,000 square feet home up to family and friends. Her home was on very high ground maybe thirty or forty feet above sea level. It was not a bad place to wait out the storm and it was relatively safe. We planned to stay there until it was safe to return to Pass Christian.

Catherine, Pass Christian, Mississippi
I debated whether or not to evacuate for this storm, even though I had boarded up my beachfront home. I knew that a hurricane was approaching because I had been watching the news every day, but my interpretation was that it was going to Florida so we were going on with business as usual. On Saturday, we realized that the hurricane had changed its course, and that day, the governor [of Mississippi] issued a mandatory evacuation saying that everyone had to leave by noon Sunday because now the storm was going to hit our area. My cousin, who is a state trooper, called me because he knew I lived on the beach. He said, "Get out, and I mean get out now." He said the only way to go was west because everything else was closed. So, I put some blankets, about three changes of clothes in my car. I didn't take anything else because I knew I had to leave. I went to my cousin the state trooper's house knowing that he would steer me

appropriately. I stayed over there Saturday night. He told me and his wife we had to leave that Sunday morning. So we got in the car. This is the honest truth. We got in the car and we drove to the Highway 10 exit, and we were like, "Where can we go?" I said, "Well, let's just pray," because we just didn't have a clue. She had a son that was an hour away in Hattiesburg, but we knew we couldn't go that way because all the roads were bumper-to-bumper. So we just sat there and prayed for a while, because we just didn't know what to do. So we prayed and we felt like we were supposed to go to Atlanta, because my daughter was in Atlanta and her mother was in Atlanta with her sister, who has a huge home, so there was adequate space for her to stay there. We knew that the spirit of the Lord had spoken to us and that we were supposed to go to Atlanta. There was no question about that. So we said, okay. Atlanta it is. The route to Atlanta was to go over to Mobile and then up to Montgomery, and then over to Atlanta. That way we would miss the Florida traffic. That route was not congested. It was a clear passage. We got to Atlanta that Sunday night safely. I knew I could stay with my daughter and her husband in Atlanta until it was safe to go home.

The narratives of these Mississippi Black women survivors of Hurricane Katrina show how they remained level-headed in order to plan and get things accomplished in spite of the pressure of the impending storm. Their characteristics embody the tenets described by Womanist theorists (Phillips, 2006; Weems, 1994; Walker, 1983), such as family activists who communicated with and convinced family members to leave or stay put as Katrina approached. These women accomplished major tasks such as securing their homes or locating places of safety for themselves during uncertain days and hours before the storm. In addition, these women survivors faced life-threatening dilemmas, and their actions parallel characteristics found in Black women of the nineteenth and twentieth century during their struggle for freedom, survival, and prosperity in the face of overt oppression and opposition (Phillips, 2006; Hines, King, and Reed, 1995; Weems, 1994; Thornton-Dill, 1988; Giddings, 1985; Walker, 1983). What's more, these Mississippi Black women used their social and cultural capital (Bourdieu, 2009; Bowser, 2007; Burt, 1997; Landry, 1987) to secure their homes and those of their friends and family. Likewise, their kinship (Collins, 1998) networks provided valuable information and assistance that enabled them to navigate the labyrinth of impending danger to find safe havens in the face of the natural disaster. Similar to the traits of Black women of the past (Patillo-McCoy, 2000; Collins, 1998; Hines, King, and Reed, 1995; Giddings, 1985), these women strove to preserve not only their safety and possessions, but also those of family and friends in the communities in which they lived. Although these women survivors escaped the hurricane's immediate catastrophic danger, their return in the aftermath of Katrina's destruction of the Mississippi Gulf Coast would leave them with only moderate provisions personally and professionally in the days ahead. The next chapter will discuss what the women found after Hurricane Katrina when they returned to the Mississippi Gulf Coast.

CHAPTER 4
KATRINA WAS TERRIBLE: RETURNING HOME AFTER THE DISASTER

ON AUGUST 29, 2005, at seven a.m., the National Hurricane Center (2005) issued an advisory, which warned that Hurricane Katrina would make her second landfall and hit the city of Bay St. Louis, Mississippi, which is less than forty-five miles from Biloxi.

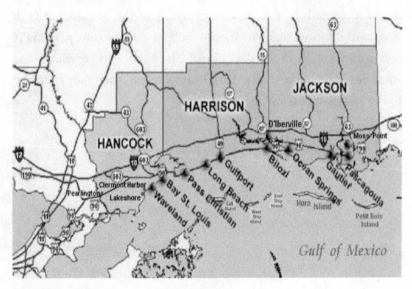

The map shows the proximity of the cities on the Mississippi Gulf Coast—three (3) counties and nine (9) cities.

The National Hurricane Center stated further that the storm was extremely dangerous ". . . with hurricane force wind gusts occurring over most of the Chandeleur Islands [thirty miles south of Biloxi] with sustained wind gusts of over 125 mph" (NOAA, 2005). Hurricane Katrina's powerful thrust into the Gulf of Mexico caused colossal damage to coastal cities and neighborhoods. This chapter will discuss what these Mississippi Black women encountered immediately after Katrina, including the loss of assets and/or damage to their homes. Fortunately, Hurricane Katrina made landfall in Mississippi during daylight; this enabled the damage the storm left to be seen the same day by those who were still on the Gulf Coast.

While most of the women in this study were miles away from danger that Monday, August 29th, two of the women decided to stay because of their commitment to family. One woman waited for her son to get off work and found that it was not safe to leave after he arrived. The other woman obeyed the wishes of her father, who refused to leave his home. Therefore, the first section of this chapter uses narrative theory to chronicle the experiences of the two women who endured Katrina's wrath as she gyrated over and describe what they saw after the storm subsided. The second section of the chapter empowers the women who evacuated to describe what they found when they returned to the Mississippi Gulf Coast after Katrina, through the lens of narrative theory. In both sections, the women describe actions that are core tenets of Womanism, which will be discussed in detail at the end of this chapter. [The photographs below show some of Hurricane Katrina's damage in Mississippi (Fitzhugh, Wilson, and Tarter, 2006). All photographs from *Sun Herald: Katrina Before & After 2005*.]

Highway 90, Pass Christian, Mississippi after Hurricane Katrina 2005.

Gulfport, Mississippi neighborhood after Katrina 2005.

Remains of the Gulfport shipyard, Gulfport, Mississippi.

Before and after of a beachfront mansion, Biloxi, Mississippi.

Remains of Gulfport Baptist Church.

Remains of McDonalds.

Remains of IHOP restaurant, Biloxi, Mississippi.

Remains of Business District, downtown Gulfport, Mississippi.

BILOXI - OCEAN SPRINGS BRIDGE

The first bridge linking people from Biloxi to Ocean Springs was a toll span that opened in 1930 and was dedicated as the nation's longest World War I monument, at 4,200 feet of it. After 32 years, though, the two-lane was turned into a fishing pier and replaced with a new bridge just to the south of it. That bridge, also claimed by Katrina, opened in May 1962 with a $7 million price tag, and was repaired seven years later after Camille. The new bridge is tentatively scheduled to be finished March 2008.

Before and after Katrina, bridge from Biloxi to Pass Christian.

Laura is the mother who, rather than evacuate without her adult son who was working, chose to ride the storm out in her three-bedroom home with him. She describes the experience of surviving Hurricane Katrina as "a Blessing."

Laura, Gulfport, Mississippi
The intense rain started about seven p.m. Sunday night and got worse throughout the night. The wind was really fierce and the rain just beat down on the roof so hard all night long. The TV went off Monday about seven a.m. We had a battery-operated radio so we could hear what was going on as people called in describing the storm until the station went off the air later that morning. After that, all we could do was pray. Katrina's howling winds and hard rain are beyond full description. It was more than scary. When the shingles blew off my roof, it caused some of the ceiling in the house to get wet and after about an hour the ceilings in the master bedroom and both bathrooms caved in, they just gave way. The water started coming in heavy in the master bathroom, which is adjacent to my laundry room. Honestly, I wasn't sure we would survive. Really, it is a miracle that we are alive today. After the ceiling caved in the bedroom, I had to move to the living room, which was the furthest point from the damaged right side of my house, but because of the ten-feet high ceiling in that room, I was still very scared and all we could do was pray and hope to survive this awful storm. After nearly eight long hours of no electricity, fierce, whipping winds, and pounding rain and hail, the storm started to slow down. Eventually, the rough wind stopped blowing and there was only steady rain. Finally, there was an eerie silence because the whistling of the wind had been so intense—it just became quiet and still—even though the storm had raged all day. It was just really strange because

it had been so[oo] bad. After a while, my son and I decided to walk outside to see what it looked like out there. The scene was unbelievable! The rain stopped and the sun was peeking through the clouds, but the area looked like it had been hit by a bomb. We saw a few standing trees and a lot of branches that had been broken off trees. Debris and tree limbs were everywhere. There were down[ed] power lines, boards of wood, and broken glass everywhere. The day was so pretty and sunny. It was as if Hurricane Katrina had never happened, but the destruction from the storm was all around us. It just didn't make sense [in a low voice] that the sun was shining so beautifully. The neighborhood was in shambles. It was just so bad [voice breaking]. After carefully walking over debris to look at the damage outside of my house, my son and I tried to make calls on our cell phones, but they still were not working. So we started to text relatives to let them know that we were alive and the storm had been really [emphasis added] bad. When the master bedroom's ceiling fell in, I decided to wait until the storm was over before sending text messages to relatives because it was just so bad and I wanted to make sure we would be okay. It's a miracle we made it with no physical injuries.

Betty, from Gulfport, is the only other woman in this study who bore the brunt of Hurricane Katrina because her father refused to leave the house he built, insisting that it withstood Hurricane Camille in 1969 and would withstand this storm too.

Betty, Gulfport, Mississippi
Since I grew up on the Coast, I have always been a storm watcher, and I had been following this storm pretty closely as it moved. Honestly, [laughing] I think I was a meteorologist in another life. Anyway, I had gone to sleep that Saturday

night and woke up at about four o'clock in the morning and realized how intense the storm had gotten so I started calling my brothers and sisters. I told them, you've got to get out of here! You've got to get your kids and you need to go! Just get out of here! I sent everybody else in the family off, and my husband (even though we were not married at the time) stayed here with my dad to weather the storm out. Going through Katrina was a traumatic experience. [She lowered her voice.] The thing that was horrible for me was the sound of the wind. It was just horrible! I was just like Lord, if for five minutes I could stop hearing this noise. It lasted twelve continuous hours. It was like standing behind a jet engine. The wind was horrible! There was just a constant howling—howling of the wind. Even though the storm was not completely over, I went outside to check to see how things were outside and to look around. The houses in my neighborhood were all still standing, but there were a lot of trees down. There was a lot of damage, but the houses were all standing and intact. Now before I went outside, I was listening to the radio station, at the time I was working at X [one of the main urban stations on the Coast]. One of the girls that worked with me [at the radio station] had an arrangement, because my parent was elderly, whenever we had a storm she would work at the station and I stayed home with my parent. When the storm was over, I would go and check on her house and see if everything was okay or let her know what was wrong. That's how we had teamed up over the years. So, I thought, let me go and check on her house. Now I had not watched TV since the power was out, so I did not know what the rest of the world had seen on TV, and I did not realize at that time how bad the storm had been. Really, I shouldn't have been out because the storm wasn't quite over yet. Anyway, when I went to check on her house, her entire neighborhood was gone! It was literally gone—it was not there anymore! I remember running down the street on top of boards, refrigerators, and whatever—trying to find her house. Then my husband (we weren't even married at the time) said to me, "STOP! STOP! There may be nails." Next, we smelled gas. Then I realized as I looked around that there was nothing. The entire neighborhood was gone. As far as I could see there was just nothing. I said we've got to get to the radio station. We turned around and went in the opposite direction and when we got to Pass Road [a main street four-way throughway in Gulfport] I could see Bayou Bernard, which was about a fourth of a mile out of its banks [Bayou Bernard is a main tributary from the Gulf of Mexico]. At that moment I realized that I couldn't get any further north. I said, "I have to go to the radio station." I didn't know if they were dead or alive after seeing that. You see, they stayed on the air longer than anybody else. They went off the air a little bit after twelve noon Monday. I said, oh my God, are we the only ones in our neighborhood who survived? I think that was the first time that it really hit me. I came back home and said, Daddy, it's really, really, really bad. I remember just trying to do an assessment of all the people in the neighborhood because a lot of people in the neighborhood were elderly. This is the neighborhood that I grew up in and I thought, what do I need to do for them? I think I went into caretaker mode [slightly laughing] or survival mode. My husband and I (as I said, we weren't married at the time) but he came to stay with my dad and I because he was worried about us staying by ourselves. We just started cooking on the grill and feeding the people. Eventually, we were able to find out that the people at the radio station were okay. God was really good, because for some reason, my cell phone worked. I had to charge it in my car because we didn't have electricity. So, people would just give me phone numbers and say just tell my family that I am okay. So I called friends and family members to let them know that, 'so and so was okay.' See there was very little communication at the time. It gave me something to do and it made me feel like, okay, I have a reason to be here.

The women's description of Hurricane Katrina as it moved over the Mississippi Gulf Coast captures its unimaginable intensity. Their comments about the sound of the wind and rain for over eight hours are similar to those of women who evacuated, as will be described in the next section of this chapter. In addition, both women listened to the local Black radio station, which dominated the airwaves in communities of color until the signal was lost. It must have been unfathomable to lose the only source of communication with the outside world as Katrina moved with ferocity over the Mississippi Gulf Coast—but both women's spirituality grounded them and served as a source of hope until the storm passed. Other Womanist themes these women mentioned, in addition to the destruction in their neighborhood, cell phone problems, and being overlooked, will be discussed in the next section, as well as the evacuation process of the remaining women.

As mentioned, ten women evacuated and returned to the region. Narrative theory allows the women to describe their experiences and the devastation that they found when they returned to their neighborhoods in their own words. Womanist tenets capture their orientation, responses to the damage they found, and speak to how they comported themselves, especially during the initial interviews, which sometimes included sadness and long pauses to collect themselves. All of the women's homes were damaged, and three survivor's houses were completely destroyed by Katrina. But, in spite of their circumstances, these women survivors were determined to "Keep Hope Alive" and move forward.

Ellen lived in a vibrant long-standing community, Back Bay, on the Western side of Biloxi, known as a well-to-do neighborhood by locals. Ellen and her husband first evacuated to his hometown in Canton, Mississippi (three hours inland), but because they lost electricity in that home, they decided to go farther inland to her hometown of Booneville, Mississippi, six hours away from Biloxi on the northern tip of the state. They left the Sunday before Katrina hit, to let the storm pass as they had many times, but their return after Katrina would change their lives permanently.

Ellen, Biloxi, Mississippi
I had talked to people who weathered the storm and I knew that Katrina had been really bad, but it was not until a week after the hurricane that I found out how the storm really affected my husband and me. When we got out of the car and walked over the rubble in our neighborhood. There were missing houses everywhere and only frames of others. There was debris everywhere. We saw everything that used to be in houses from washing machines to bedroom furniture, clothes hanging on bare tree branches to baby strollers. Just give me a minute. [She paused for about five seconds to collect herself.] See, I lost my home, cars, and everything inside my home. There was only a frame of our home standing but everything inside was destroyed. [Her voice dropped.] We had left two cars in the garage and they were twenty feet from our house on one side. One of the cars was an antique my husband was restoring—it was a mess and the other car had been tossed and was eventually totaled. My daughter was with us and all she could do was cry. It was just terrible. [Her voice dropped again.] There were down[ed] trees everywhere in the neighborhood. My husband was strong for all of us. Although the frame of our house was there, we were homeless after Katrina. [Ellen's voice dropped

and she was silent for a few seconds.] We stayed with my daughter in her home in Mobile, Alabama, until we could figure out what to do next. During this time, my husband and I drove about an hour and a half back and forth from Mobile to Gulfport, in heavy traffic for a few months to work. We had long days. We left at about four o'clock in the morning and got home late every night. My job offered us temporary shelter in a dormitory to make things a little easier for us, but it took us about six months to get a FEMA trailer placed in front of our destroyed home.

Two days before Hurricane Katrina hit, Jeanette, a woman from Pass Christian, and her husband evacuated to Hattiesburg, Mississippi, a one-hour drive from the Gulf Coast.

Jeanette, Pass Christian, Mississippi

We stayed in the hotel that Saturday night. It was raining pretty hard and the wind was fierce too. On Sunday afternoon, a friend we knew came to look for us at the hotel because we had trailed her to Hattiesburg. Our friend, Ms. M, was staying there with one of her associates. My friend's associate was the executive director of a private school which was opened in 1923 by an African-American Methodist bishop, which sits on six hundred acres in Waveland. After a brief introduction and conversation, her friend's associate invited me and Joe [Jeanette's husband] to come to her home to wait the storm out with them rather than stay in the hotel. We got our stuff from the hotel, got in Joe's Jaguar, and followed them to the executive director's "Southern Glory" style home in Hattiesburg. The storm was vicious and raging. So, in hindsight, we were glad to be there because her home was very secure. On Tuesday, after Katrina, we were listening to a battery-powered radio when we learned that the Mississippi Gulf Coast had bore the brunt of the hurricane. The executive director started making calls to her state official friends and learned that only essential personnel were allowed to access Highway 90 because it was impassable by regular vehicles. After talking to a few people, the executive director was able to plan a visit that Friday, September 2 [four days after Katrina] to the area where [the private school] was located, but officials told her that the place was a total loss. Because we were at the executive director's home, we got a chance to go with her to view the damage on the Mississippi Gulf Coast, [the private school], and our home. Really, it was a blessing to be able to go back to check on our property with her because it was unsafe and they were not allowing most people back into the area right then. We were beyond belief at the havoc caused by Hurricane Katrina. It was just unbelievable! So many homes were totally demolished. On one plot of land you could tell that the whole house or business imploded because there was timber and pieces of wood piled up three or four feet high. Debris was everywhere! You couldn't tell where one street stopped and another started. As we drove through Pass Christian, the infrastructure of the city was nonexistent. So many businesses were wiped out—GONE [emphasis intended]! Only shells were visible. It was like a bomb or an explosion had blasted in the area. The enormity of the storm was just beyond belief even though we saw it with our own eyes. It is still mind-boggling! The site of [the private school] was so sad. All of the buildings on the property were washed away. There was nothing left but a flat, desert-looking land mass of lumber and broken trees. One hundred percent (100%) of Black history was gone. [The private school] had survived Camille, but not Hurricane Katrina. When we got to our neighborhood and saw our house still standing, we were so relieved, but we saw dangling shutters, broken glass, a slightly opened front door, and an open empty garage. Thank God, we only had one car at that time or it would have been ruined. And I will never forget seeing three feet of mud inside my house. It was disgusting and I got angry! I was too mad to cry right then. As mad as I was, I knew we were fortunate and had a place to start again from, even though the place was a mess. The aftermath of Katrina was a very unpleasant and unbelievable sight to see.

Another woman, Sam from Pass Christian, who evacuated on the Sunday before Katrina slammed into the Mississippi Gulf Coast, describes her experience next:

Sam, Pass Christian, Mississippi
My family and I had evacuated to my niece's house inland in Kiln, Mississippi [which is one hour west of the Gulf Coast]. As a part of the management team, I had to work the Saturday before the storm. My niece opened her 8,000 sq. ft. home to family and friends. Her home was on very high ground, maybe thirty or forty feet above sea level. It was not a bad place to wait out the storm since we had to and it was a relatively safe distance from the beach. But that was still one of the worst mistakes of my life. You see, I wanted to go further inland, but we decided to go there after it had gotten so late in the day. The night before and day of Katrina was a traumatic experience for all of us because the wind was blowing so hard. It was just whipping and howling. It was raining and hailing so hard on the roof. It was a very scary experience that we hoped would end, but the storm was intense and did not slow down. After about eight to ten hours that day, the raging storm started to subside, and we started to hear from different people about how bad the

storm had been on the battery-operated radio. People were calling in from different areas on the Gulf Coast, but we never heard a word or got a report about Pass Christian, and in my mind, I thought if no one has said a word about Pass Christian—that is not good! If nobody has said anything about Pass Christian, it must be very badly devastated. We were all in one room, and after the storm died down, the men in the house said we are going to go out and look around. They tried to go to the interstate but, of course, it was closed because there were fallen light poles, trees, and everything else across the road. You see, we were kind of in a rural area. There were some other people in the neighborhood who teamed up with my two brothers, his colleagues from Louisiana, and my two grown sons. The neighborhood men said they were going to go to get our equipment and move this debris. The men in our family assisted with that. Then the men drove down to Pass Christian. When they came back, they said you can't go there. And I said I'm going there! We're going there! Then my sister-in-law, my daughter-in-law, my niece, and I got in the car and, of course, they drove us but it was like driving through an obstacle course because seventy-five percent of the roads were closed and you couldn't pass down the street because houses were in the middle of the street, but somehow we made it. My house was one of the few homes still standing. There were about 5,000 people who lived in Pass Christian before the storm, and seventy-five percent of the homes were totally gone. I was one of the few fortunate ones who had a home that was still there, but it had sustained thirty feet of water. So the water was over my house. I had a deck on the back of my house. I could see my deck in the woods about ten feet from my home. My refrigerator was at my French patio door off from my kitchen. I found a few pictures. It was really ironic. My mother died in 1997, and her picture was at the back door. I had put all my pictures in a box in the attic because I felt like they would be safe there. Before the storm, I thought to myself, well, the house is big and tall, and if we get a little water, my pictures will be safe. Well, I had no idea in my wildest dreams that the water would go over my home. I found a picture at my front door and a picture at my back door. I thought after a while, how could those pictures have gotten there? Then I thought, well, they must have floated there. Of course [voice lowered], I started crying along with everybody else because there was nothing left. Everything was just muddy and there were still four or five feet of water in my house. We couldn't go in. We were just at the door. But I had to go to see the house for myself. I wanted to go. I didn't care. Of course, when we got back, my sons said: "We didn't want you to go because it was so horrible. You don't need to see anything like that, Mom." But I said, "I wanted to go—I'm an adult—I can take it." But just seeing it—it was overwhelming! And I lived through Hurricane Camille in 1969, and I remember that time [pause], but this was nothing compared to that. This was much worse!

Catherine, from Pass Christian, described her return to the Mississippi Gulf Coast just thirty-six hours after Katrina hit.

Catherine, Pass Christian, Mississippi
My story is a little unique. I stayed with my daughter in Atlanta, and I was glued to the TV and prayed. I realized there was absolutely nothing I could do. I noticed that the few reports about Mississippi were about Biloxi and Gulfport until Robin Roberts [Robin grew up in Pass Christian] went down and reported from Pass Christian. All the reports on Pass Christian and its survivors were bleak. I called my

cousin [the Mississippi state trooper], and he told me that Pass Christian was nearly wiped off the map and all the beachfront homes were destroyed, including my 3,000 square feet condo. I was just numb. [Her voice dropped.] He said that Katrina buckled the interstate pavement and only essential personnel were allowed to access Interstate 90, which ran in front of the beach. It was unbelievable. My home was washed away by Katrina, completely leveled; there was nothing left for me to go back to because my condo was one block from the beach. It was gone. From that point on, it was just obvious—okay—everything I have is gone. This is what it is. It was unbelievable. I did not have anything to go back to after Katrina.

Catherine decided to stay in Atlanta for a while to figure out what to do next. Initially, Katrina seemed almost surreal to her. The reality hit home about a week later, as she watched television.

Catherine, Pass Christian, Mississippi
I was in Atlanta at my daughter's house where I evacuated to after the hurricane empathizing about the plight of the Katrina survivors on TV and my daughter looked at me and said: "Mama, you are one of those poor people who lost their home and everything that they owned." After that, I started the process of getting my business in order with the insurance company and the agencies that helped Hurricane Katrina survivors in the Atlanta area. It was two months later before I visited the site where my home once stood in Pass Christian. And that was a very sad day. I saw only a concrete slab where my beachfront condo complex once stood [voice breaking]. My dream home that I worked all my life for was destroyed by Katrina in a matter of just one day. I can't fully explain how I really felt, but I knew I had to keep going forward, and I had already started that process.

Jean, Biloxi, Mississippi

After Katrina, when we went back to Biloxi where we had lived for years, I learned that our home and my business were gone. [Jean paused and sighed deeply.] I built that beauty shop clientele over the years, and it was how I took care of me and my family. See, I lost my car and everything else in the storm. That was a tough time. [Jean's voice dropped as she collected herself. Then she said,] The news don't talk about what happen here. It seems like the media think Mississippi is not right next door to New Orleans. We are only one hour from there. Hurricane Katrina hit really hard here. It was real bad, and ninety percent of the area is totally gone.

This chapter highlighted these Mississippi Black women's stories by first describing what it was like for two women who, because of unforeseen family circumstances, experienced Katrina's 200 mph wind gusts, pounding rain, and hail as she moved across the Gulf Coast. In addition, the women's narratives describe their remarkable experience of surviving Hurricane Katrina. The previous section contained eyewitness accounts of the destruction Katrina left hours, weeks, and months after the hurricane landed a devastating blow to the region. The women's striking and dramatic descriptions of what the hurricane sounded like during the storm, and what the scene immediately afterwards looked like, are surreal, yet they are true as the photographs confirm. Similarly, Ann Petry's personal survival of The Great New England hurricane of 1938 in *Country Place* (Petry, 1944), as corroborated by her daughter, Elisabeth (Petry, 2009), echo the words described by these Katrina survivors. For example, Petry's description of how the storm beat the windows like an evil spirit (p. 156), the sound of the persistent beating rain (p. 177), and the violent force of the nagging, roaring (p. 21), howling, shrieking wind (p. 176), mirror these Mississippi women's descriptions. Like Petry and Black women generationally, these Katrina women's stories depict courage, evoke emotion, and point to their Womanist outlook. In addition, the chapter discussed what the women experienced and decided to do after they returned to the Gulf Coast to begin the process of recovery. Fluidity, collectivity, spiritualism, balance, level-headedness, and dynamism are all foundational characteristics of Womanist theory—and all are present in the women's narratives, in their bravery and resolve to act after a Category 5 hurricane. The women's ability to convince family members to do what they thought was best—before and after the storm—to care for each other also shines through in their narratives.

All of the women's homes were damaged by Katrina's force. The damage ranged from moderate to severe. Three women's homes were demolished, and more than half lost part of their roofs, doors and required other external repairs. Several women had to have mud, sand, water, and debris removed from their homes. This meant that the recovery included home renovations, new appliances, and furniture to replace that which was muddy, damaged or ruined. The importance of the women's social networks, which included relatives and friends who had access to information that was shared with the women to assist their evacuation and return after the hurricane, was another salient feature of this chapter. What's more, the chapter painted vivid examples of the women's social standing, coordination, and problem-solving skills. What these Black women found upon their return to the Mississippi Gulf Coast is only one part of the story. Lastly, these stories address the fact that since 2005 during the national media's Hurricane Katrina anniversary coverage, Mississippi continues to be overlooked and rarely are survivors from the state mentioned. The next chapter will paint the picture of what these Mississippi women survivors faced after Hurricane Katrina, beginning with their descriptions of their employment dilemmas and how they worked through them.

CHAPTER 5
EMPLOYMENT AND ECONOMICS— NOW WHAT?

HURRICANE KATRINA IS ONE of the most expensive natural disasters in American history with an estimated cost of $161 billion (Unger and Ingram, 2018). Katrina's pounding 175 mph sustained wind gusts and storm surge of 11.45ft (NOAA, 2005) crashed into the state's twenty-six miles of scenic coastal beaches, leveled neighborhoods, and nearly destroyed the economic infrastructure on the Mississippi Gulf Coast. Days after the hurricane, Governor Haley Barbour declared all eighty-two counties in Mississippi a disaster area due to the storm's overwhelming destruction. All these women were impacted by the changes in the economy after the disaster. They will describe how they handled and found creative ways to work through the employment and economic changes thrust upon them by the aftermath of Hurricane Katrina.

The Gulf Coast is known as an economic engine in Mississippi because it is home to the $2.5 billion a year gambling industry (ESA, 2006). Katrina's force halted the industry's lucrative operations, damaging and destroying hotels and casinos. What is more, the hurricane destroyed the infrastructure of key Gulf Coast cities, namely Gulfport and Biloxi, and crippled smaller coastline cities like Bay St. Louis, Waveland, Pass Christian, Ocean Springs, and

Pascagoula (Fitzhugh, Wilson, and Tarter, 2006), which comprise the Gulf Coast counties Harrison and Hancock, where the women in this study lived.

Before the storm, the unemployment rate in Hancock and Harrison county was 5.9 percent, but the figure nearly quadrupled to between 22 percent to 24.3 percent one month after Katrina (DOL, 2015, DOL, 2006). The Quarterly Census on Employment and Wages (ILS, 2007) showed that the most extensive job losses—more than 127,000—were on the Mississippi Gulf Coast in Harrison County (Census, 2006). Since Hurricane Katrina caused major damage to the infrastructure on the Mississippi Gulf Coast, this significantly impacted the employment status of residents in the region and the women in this study. In fact, half of these women were employed at small businesses, which made up a large part of the economy on the Coast. Since only a few studies (Lovell, 2014; Taylor & Silver, 2006; Whelan, 2006; Jones-DeWeever & Hartman, 2006) highlight the economic effect of Katrina survivors, this longitudinal study sheds light upon and provides missing data on Hurricane Katrina survivors' economic quandary. None of the studies examine in depth the plight of Mississippi Hurricane Katrina survivors. Therefore, this chapter will discuss the job standing of these Mississippi women before and after Hurricane Katrina and analyze how they handled their employment dilemmas.

In Mississippi, tourism is a major source of income. After Tunica, another site of gaming in the state, Harrison County generates the second largest casino revenue for the state and speaks to the impact of the industry on the Gulf Coast. This is important because throughout the interviews several women referred to tourism and the casinos, although only one of the women worked in the industry. Gender disparity in employment is well known. Mississippi has the thirteenth biggest gender pay gap in the United States, with women in full-time jobs earning, on average 23.1 percent less than men (Hess, 2019).

The average annual income for women in Mississippi before Katrina was $25,736 (ACS, 2006). According to the American Community Survey (2006), nearly 41,000 of the women who lived on the Gulf Coast had "some" college experience and an average salary of $21,630 (Demographics, 2005). It is worth noting that only eighteen percent of Harrison County females have college experience (ACS, 2006). Because ten of these Black women are college graduates and the others fit the category described by the ACS (2006), this makes their educational attainment above average and is representative of their economic status. In Harrison County, women college graduates' income was $36,250 (ACS, 2006). Due to privacy and confidentiality, the women's incomes in this study are not reported, but the types of positions and work experience suggest that their salaries fit within or are likely higher than Mississippi's average salary range for college graduates. Since education is one of the key indicators of obtaining the best jobs and higher salaries, it is not surprising that these factors are conflated with disaster survivors' ability to recover (Neumayer & Plumper, 2007).

Prior to Hurricane Katrina, all of the women in this study held full-time middle or senior management positions. Most of these professional women had worked over ten years in their careers [see the chart below]. Some of the positions these women held were: school teacher, manager of administration at Job Corps, manager in a nursing home, radio personality, congressional representative, independent licensed social worker, vice president of human resources, and hair salon owner.

WOMEN'S OCCUPATIONS BEFORE HURRICANE KATRINA

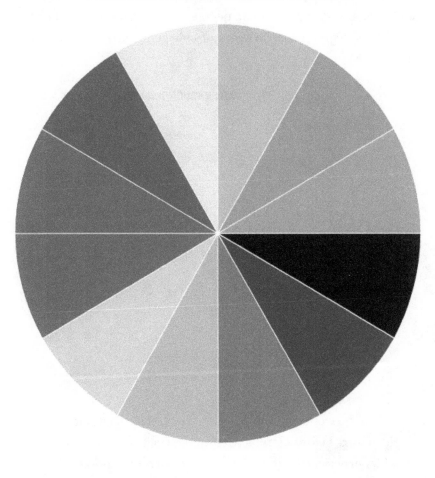

- Social Worker MSW/LICSW
- VP/Casino
- State Representative
- Manager Job Corps
- Manager Radio Station
- Owner- Hair Salon
- Manager Community Service Org
- Manager State Agency
- Manager Nursing Home
- School Teacher
- Administrator Utilities company
- Bank Administrator

As mentioned, all of the women, except two, had college degrees, and several had post-graduate degrees. The two women without a bachelor's degree had two years of college experience [see chart below].

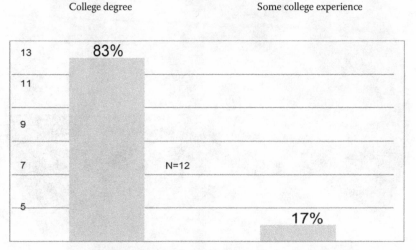

MISSISSIPPI WOMEN'S EDUCATION LEVEL

College degree   Some college experience

50% of the women had a Master's degree before Katrina.

All of the women in this study held positions of authority in the world of work before Katrina. After the storm, the women used their training, experiences, and Womanist acumen to maintain stability and begin the recovery process. Katrina's damage to the Mississippi Gulf Coast's infrastructure brought the economy to a near standstill. According to Whelan (2006), this was the primary issue after Katrina. For weeks, the interstate and roads were impassable. There were very few retail stores or restaurants open to the public after the disaster. A *Fortune* magazine article said that Walmart was one of the region's only lifelines (Devin, 2005), and a local newspaper, the *Sun Herald*, reported that many residents remember Waffle House doors remained open after Katrina (Mitchell, 2016). In Mississippi, small businesses made up a large part of the Gulf Coast economy, and the loss of these businesses was hard and took a toll on the region. Many businesses were forced to reorganize, right-size, or close permanently. This precipitated an employment crisis for many disaster survivors, including the women in this study, causing changes in their lives as revealed in their responses to questions about their job status before and after the storm. Despite the dilemmas the women faced, their stories are inspiring and illustrate the types of position and level of responsibility they held before and after Katrina. Next, narrative theory provides a lens through which the women are given agency to tell their poignant employment experiences. Now, the women will discuss their situations.

Catherine, Pass Christian, Mississippi

Before Katrina, I worked as a social worker for forty years. You see, I had opened my own business, and I was a contracted worker at a retirement home for seniors with Alzheimer's. I enjoyed the job because I had clients from all over the country. I worked at the agency until late Friday night before the storm because the owners had to evacuate all of the patients to safe quarters and I was in a quasi-management role. After Katrina, my business was gone. I lost everything. There was nothing left but a slab where my office used to be. It was gone, just like my beachfront home... After the hurricane, while I was in Atlanta, I [started getting] unemployment because I knew how [to do that], because I had helped so many clients get unemployment over the years. I found myself helping and praying for people while I was waiting in the lines for services. I tried to encourage people and started singing. Other people joined me as we waited. It felt good.

Catherine smiled broadly as she told this part of her story. It was evident that she was happy she was able to use her social work background and training to support herself and to help and encourage other Katrina survivors. Catherine continued:

Before Katrina, I went to church in New Orleans at one of the large nationally known ministries. As I watched TV in Atlanta, I constantly heard the leaders say that they wanted to know how people were doing and to help people. You see, [Catherine said proudly] they knew me, and that I lived on the beach, had a thriving business, and all of that. So I sent them an email and told them that I was doing fine and that I had evacuated and was in Atlanta. I also told them I wanted to help too. [I said] if there was anything that I could do to help them, I would do it because I really wanted to come back. You see the authorities were not allowing people back at that time. [Catherine is referring to the first few weeks after Katrina.] A ministry leader called me and said that they would send for me and let me help run [manage] a place that they were starting [where people could get assistance] after the storm. They called it the Compassion Center. I packed my car and drove to Louisiana during the middle of September right before my birthday on September 3 to start that job. The ministry had turned a gym into a distribution center and gave people donations that they had received from all over the world. My job was to counsel and help people, just meet their needs. The ministry welcomed me and really took care of me. They gave me a salary, probably one tenth of what my normal salary would have been, but they were taking good care of me. If someone came into the Compassion Center upset and crying, of course I would talk to them. I worked there from September to December. At the beginning of the new year, they closed the Compassion Center and offered me a job with the ministry. Well really, they ordained me as a minister because they knew I had my

Masters and was working on my Doctorate. In 2006, they gave me a salaried position in the ministry, which was an increase in my salary, but nothing like what I was used to, but anyway, that's what I did. Then I moved into an apartment on my own and became self-sufficient. But I really didn't want to live in New Orleans. It was just a place [that] I liked to visit. So in 2007, I decided to resign from my job, travel to Israel, and move back to Atlanta when I returned [from Israel] because the [Mississippi] Gulf Coast was still struggling to rebound, but that was where I really wanted to be.

Catherine's story introduces a theme that is present in the narratives of other women in this study, which is a fluctuation in their salary before and after Hurricane Katrina. Although the actual salaries of these women are kept confidential due to privacy issues, like Catherine, half of these women discussed the reduction of income in their jobs after Katrina as opposed to their pre-Katrina salary. Also, Catherine mentioned the trip to Israel that she took with a portion of her insurance settlement. Catherine said she traveled with some of the money in 2007 because she needed time to just relax. Catherine eventually resumed her career as a licensed social work contractor in Mississippi.

Sam, Pass Christian, Mississippi

You see, before the storm I had a job with a hospitality company. I was on the top management team for one of the largest casinos in America. I was the vice president of human resources. When we got the forty-eight-hour notice that Katrina was heading our way, I had to work because we had to close the business. After Katrina, I kept my job for a few months because we had a disaster relief office for our employees since Katrina shut down all the casinos for a period of time. I was offered the opportunity to go to another property because there are many locations across the country, but I chose not to do that. Some of my colleagues were worried about me and my decision. But you know what I told them? I said, I have never had this much clarity in my entire life. I don't have a job, and I don't have a home to stay in right now, but I have peace. And I knew that my needs would be taken care of. You see, I knew that—that job was not my source. I realized what's important and what's not important. Making six figures [is not], if I don't have a life, if I don't have family, it's just not that important. When I had the opportunity to go back to that job or move to another location, I told them, I can't do that. I know I can't go back to that rat race. I can't go back to working sixty or seventy hours a week. I was not living! I was just going through the motions. It's just not worth it; there is just more to life than that. I want to spend time with my sons and grandkids. I want to do more things in my community. That's just not how God intended for us to live our lives or the purpose he made us for—work, work, work. So I decided I would apply for positions in local government. I thought that was the place I could make the biggest impact, and trust me, it has truly been an experience. The break between jobs gave me a chance to get my bearings. When I got the call from the CEO of one of the largest cities on the Coast, I told [his administrative assistant] that I had been waiting on her call. You see, I'm a little bit aggressive, not assertive. [Sam smiled broadly.] After that, I went on a trip to Arizona to visit my son, who had temporarily moved out there after he and his wife lost their house after Katrina, but they are back here now. While I was there, I told them that I had to hurry up and get back because I am getting ready to go to work. He said, "Mom, how do you know you will get the job?" I told him, I just know I am going to get the job. The next week I had the committee interview and [a key leader] interviewed me too. [Sam smiled proudly and in a matter-of-fact manner.] They called me back and said when can you start? I've been there since 2010. That was three years ago. My position is appointed by [a key leader], and my longevity depends on who's in office. I have made significant changes since I have been in the position. I think I will have a job for a while [smiling confidently]. Coming from a private to public job was really different. One day I said to myself, God really has a sense of humor because he has taken a Type-A personality and put her in one of the slowest industries ever. So I said, okay, Sam, they are not going to change so you are going to have to change your tactics a little bit.

It was evident as Sam spoke about her work situation that she was a proud and driven woman who had become successful personally and economically. She beamed with confidence and spoke compellingly about the positions of authority she held in the private and public sector.

Joanne, Gulfport, Mississippi
Before the hurricane, I had a very good job, but it's like, I lost everything in one day. My past employer tried to get me to come back to my great job, but I chose not to go back. I needed a calm time—some time for me. My family is priority. I have changed and am still figuring it out, but I know I will get another job in the future.

Within six months, Joanne and all of the women had found new full-time jobs, although some of the new occupations were not at the management level they had prior to the storm.

Jean, Biloxi, Mississippi

Well, before Hurricane Katrina, I worked as a cosmetologist for twenty-one years, but my shop went down with the storm. . . . Thank God, my girlfriend contacted me and told me—if I wanted a job I could come to Houston and work for her temp agency. Of course, I went. I was in Houston for three months and worked as an administrative clerk at her temp agency, but I decided I wanted to come back to Biloxi. So, after figuring out where I would stay, I left Houston for home [Biloxi]. After coming back, [another] friend told me about a meeting where women met to talk about what was going on and what we could do to help people and especially women who so desperately needed help like affordable housing, senior services, and childcare after the storm. I agreed to attend the women's meeting if my friend would pick me up. I knew I was not going to just sit there on the sidelines and wait to see if anything would happen. I knew I had to do something [Jean said emphatically]! First, I became the secretary of the group. Eventually, one thing led to another, and I became the leader of the group.

And, all of a sudden, I ended up in a whole new realm of work. Now I am the executive director of. . . [a woman's organization]. I never thought that I would be doing this [type of work] before Katrina. We are still going strong today, even though we don't get all the support we need. We started out with twenty-one women who were committed to our vision for the community, and we know our voices need to be heard as decisions are made. See, there is still a lot that needs to be done because so many people lost their jobs after Katrina. Honestly, I think the way we need to go is green jobs and propose a way for citizens on the Gulf Coast to be hired by environmentally friendly companies. So, at my agency, we are lobbying for green jobs. The Coast [has always been] known as an entertainment region, and the casinos were among the largest employers before the storm. But since most of the ships were damaged or destroyed, there are fewer people working for the casinos, besides the fact that many people don't like working on the boats. I think people need to get educated and trained as soon as possible to do that green job work. I think that could be one of the answers to help the region continue to recover. I really do [Jean said emphatically]! See, employment is still a big problem for many people on the coast.

Jean's career change and leadership role has empowered her to serve the Gulf Coast community in a very different and important way since Katrina. The start-up now pays her salary and that of several other full-time workers, all of whom are women. Also, she and the agency have received support from several national women's organizations and continue to actively serve the community. Jean's account parallels Catherine's narrative by highlighting the fact that these women wanted to return to the Mississippi Gulf Coast even though they had job opportunities in other states. This speaks to the Womanist principle of collectivism, as they longed for the familiarity of their community, family, and friends. Ultimately, both women gave up their jobs and returned to Mississippi after making living arrangements without definitive employment plans. As time passed, both Jean and Catherine found employment to reestablish themselves on the Mississippi Gulf Coast where they live today.

Laura, Gulfport, Mississippi
I worked as one of the managers at a senior citizens' home before Katrina. After the storm, I learned that the senior citizens' home was severely damaged and would not reopen. So I lost my job, and that was personally very difficult for

me. [Laura paused briefly.] I felt that they [the owners of the agency] should have been more understanding and concerned about their employees, but they let people go because that's what [they thought] was best for the business. But you know things like that happen and you just move on. After thinking about my situation for a week or two, and talking to family and friends, I decided that I was going to go and get me a FEMA job; and that's exactly what I did. I worked for FEMA until the government right-sized the mission last year [2010]. I have had two different jobs since Katrina. Now, in my third job, I work at a bank in a staff position. Although I have found three full-time jobs since the storm, FEMA was the only job I have had at the same salary that I had before Katrina. I have not been able to find a permanent position at the management level. But I won't stop looking for one. [Laura smiled.]

Laura's story introduces the theme of underemployment, which was mentioned by Catherine and other women in this study. Jean's comments on this issue are telling. She said, "we have people who are qualified to do things, but they are not hiring them. They say you are overqualified, so you lower your standards, but they still don't hire you. It's a catch-22." Over half of these women survivors have worked in jobs beneath their experience level and received lower salaries than the ones that they had before the hurricane. Only three of them have been able to find a job at the same level or salary that they had prior to the storm. Despite being underemployed, like Laura, most of the women were thankful for employment and hopeful of finding better jobs at the management level, like the ones that they had prior to Katrina.

In addition, Laura's story introduces the issue of community and personal well-being over business interests. Three-fourths of the women argued that a key driver of post-Katrina policy and business decisions should be concern for the wellbeing of family, neighbors, friends, and community. This kind of collectivism is one of the bulwarks of Womanist theory. Laura's words mirror those of others in this study: "We are in this together now, because Katrina leveled the playing field for all of us, at least."

Lynne, Biloxi, Mississippi
I worked as a school teacher before Katrina, but I lost my job after the storm. [Many school buildings were destroyed and damaged after Katrina, which led to school closures, diminished student enrollment, and teacher cutbacks.] A few weeks after Katrina, FEMA advertised on the radio that they were looking for people to do various types of work, so I called the number and left my contact information but never heard anything back from them. One day while I was at a community center, I found out that they had a place where people who lost their jobs as a result of Hurricane Katrina could apply for unemployment. So, since I hadn't found another teaching position, I went to that section at the community center to apply for unemployment. FEMA had a room in that section too. After talking with the woman at FEMA briefly, she asked me if I wanted a job. At first, I thought that she thought I was someone else. Then she explained what they did and asked me again if I wanted a job. I said, well, yes [in an upbeat tone], I'll take an application.

The rising inflection in Lynne's voice, as she said, *"Well, yes. . . "* captured the hopeful anticipation of getting a job she must have felt that day.

Lynne continued:

I sat down and filled out the application then took it back up to the desk [with surprise in her voice]. According to the paperwork, I was hired on that day. I started working the next week. It's not a permanent position, but it's better than nothing because so many people still need jobs right now.

Lynne's description of her experience is similar to most of the women in this study. In spite of what they had experienced, they took a personally proactive stance after Katrina and exhibited confidence by going to community centers, FEMA offices, and meetings to do what they could about their employment situation. For instance, responses such as, "I'm going to go get a FEMA job," [Laura] "I knew I was not going to just sit there on the sideline," [Jean] and other comments show that these women found the wherewithal to tackle their employment situation after Katrina. Their fluidity and commitment to finding a way out of no way, personally and with the help of their networks, are fundamental aspects of Womanist ideology.

Betty, Gulfport, Mississippi
Before the storm, I worked at the radio station as an on-air personality. I continued to work at the station for about six months but eventually decided to leave that job. You see, all [with emphasis], and I mean all day long, we listened to Katrina survivors stories and gave people the best information we could on how they could get the help that they *so desperately* needed.

Betty spoke slowly and dropped her voice as she described listening to the stories. It was clear that they made her feel very sad and she wanted to help the callers.
Betty continued:

I decided I could be of better service by using my teaching degree since I am certified [to teach]. So, I accepted a full-time teaching position with an. . . [elementary school], and I am still there today.

Betty, like Jean and Catherine, as well as other women in this study, had a personal desire to assist their community. Betty chose to do this by using her teaching certificate. Like Black Womanists of the twentieth century (Hunter, 1997; Clark, King, and Reed,1995; Cooper, 1892), these women proactively drew from their personal and professional toolboxes and found ways to assist their community after Katrina with or without assistance from outside their neighborhoods.

Corene, Gulfport, Mississippi

Well, after Katrina, I retired. I had been a member of the legislature since my husband's death. [Her husband held the same state legislator's seat she was elected to after his death ten years prior to Katrina.] But I'll keep doing as much as I can for my community. I did what I could for the region before I left office, but we still have so much to do here on the Coast. See, Katrina was a monster storm, and since our region of the state depends on tourism, we need to keep opening restaurants and attracting tourists. The downtown businesses are trying to come back, but, you see, we lost so many more small businesses than large companies and that hurt our city a lot as well as individual loss of homes. The hotels on the beach and casinos are coming back and rebuilding again, but it's a slow process. Even though the Coast is not as beautiful as it was before Katrina, we need tourists to keep traveling and vacationing here. I really believe the Coast will continue to improve economically.

Corene, like Jean, Catherine, Sam, Betty, and the other women in this study, had a strong desire to be of service to their community after Katrina. Their perspectives emphasize the collective rather than individual standpoint and is a core tenet of Womanism. Moreover, Corene's statement, "I'll keep doing as much as I can for my community," and other women's comments about wanting to help echo those of twentieth century Black Womanists (Gilkes, 2001; Clark, King, and Reed, 1995; Giddings, 1985), who maintained and built their communities during Jim Crow segregation, the Civil Rights era, and present day turbulent times.

Ellen, Biloxi, Mississippi

After Katrina, I had the same job for a few months. This was a job that I had worked so hard in and that I had really given my all. I was a recruitment supervisor for [a government contractor], an independent median-sized residential educational and vocational training center before Katrina. But after three months, I was laid off from my job. See, I was in a management position, and I was thinking that this was a job that I would retire from. But it just didn't work out that way. That was really disappointing. So, because I had bills, I had to find another job. Since my bachelors is in social work, [I used] my experience and friends [to] find another job within two months. So now I am in a job that I feel is a calling. See, now I go into the homes of different families and [facilitate the process of making] positive changes in their daily lives as a family preservation counselor. This job is *really* [emphasis added] rewarding to me personally. The money and [level of the position] are very different from what I had before Katrina. This is more like an entry-level-type job, but it is very rewarding to help people every day.

Similar to other women's comments in this chapter, Ellen's narrative stresses collectivist assisting and underemployment. But the statements shed light upon and draw attention to the issue of these women's capability to manage their emotions and situations that were beyond their control. These women demonstrate their psychological health after Katrina by various comments. For example, "it just didn't work out that way" [Ellen, referring to the job from which she planned to retire]; "you just move on" [Laura, who remarked on her employers' decision to close the business]; and "I have never had more clarity in my entire life" [Sam, regarding her decision to not accept another position offered by her employer after Katrina]. These remarks, like those from others in this study, show these women's ability to effectively determine the best way for them to manage the circumstances after Katrina personally and professionally. The women examined the situation that they faced and made sound choices that would move them toward recovery after the disaster. As mentioned, the cost of cleaning up and rebuilding after Katrina is estimated at over $100 billion. This huge dollar amount paints a broad picture of the financial impact of the hurricane across the region. However, few studies have focused on the impact on employment on the Mississippi Gulf Coast, and none focus on Black women survivors' dilemma after the storm. The women's experiences provide a lens through which one can understand some of the dynamics of the economic impact of Katrina on the state.

Their social and cultural capital, such as college degrees, professional experience, and kinship networks were central to their ability to retain old jobs and obtain new ones. Because of some of the women's roles in organizations prior to Katrina, they were responsible for the closing and reopening of businesses before and after the storm. Other women in the study benefited from the help former employers provided for them and their families, such as housing and knowledge of where to get the help that they desperately needed after Katrina. Although most women faced job loss, they confidently and assertively looked for new jobs and found them. Several women made decisions that led them to new careers in different industries. This demonstrates some of the core precepts of Womanism, such as working together for the good of all people (Ogunyemi, 1985), fluidity to adjust to situations (Phillips, 2006), and ability to discover strengths by self-affirmation (Cannon, 1996, Ogunyemi, 1985).

Almost all of these women discussed their concern and/or care for people in their community. Through involvement within their community, several women ensured that all constituents' voices were heard. Another pledged to ignore retirement and continue to work. Several women thought that local businesses and big companies put profits and their organization's survival before their workers', and the region's, wellbeing in the aftermath of the storm. Most of these women found ways to be of service to their community by helping others or assisting people while waiting in long lines.

Due to privacy and confidentiality issues, their individual incomes are not provided, but the women's comments make it reasonable to believe that their salaries may have been higher than those projected by the Mississippi Institute of Higher Learning (2008) for women living in Mississippi with a Bachelor's degree. In spite of that, what these women were able to accomplish after Katrina with their incomes was ingenious and remarkable. Unfortunately, although most women have worked full-time consistently since the hurricane, their salaries are not as high as they were before Katrina. With the exception of one woman, all of them have changed jobs at least once, and most have had two or more positions since the storm. This is especially problematic for these middle-aged, college-educated, highly skilled and experienced women because they are in the prime earning years of their working lives.

Despite Hurricane Katrina's fury, these women continue to embody the will to recover and concern for their community's recovery. The next chapter will discuss and analyze the ways in which these Mississippi Black women report their gratitude and thankfulness for people and entities that helped them most after Hurricane Katrina.

CHAPTER 6
THE SUSTAINING FORCE:SOMETHING WITHIN AND ANGELS FROM GOD

HURRICANE KATRINA LEFT the Mississippi Gulf Coast in shambles. In spite of that, the women in this study were determined to make the best of things with what they had left and start the rebuilding process. This chapter will discuss what these Mississippi women survivors said was helpful to them after the hurricane and what they did to move forward.

To understand fully why support was so useful to overcome the obstacles these Mississippi women faced after the hurricane's devastation, two examples provide pictures of the disaster's magnitude in the region. First, the disaster's damage shut down the Gulf Coast's second and third largest cities, Gulfport and Biloxi, and left the city of Pass Christian and other smaller towns unrecognizable. The hurricane's force was so strong that it relocated casino barges, that averaged thirty feet and more than 15,000 pounds, over a fourth of a mile onto already badly damaged highways [see photos below]. The main thorough way, Highway 90, was impassable [see the photos below], making it almost impossible for residents to move around in their community.

Relocated remains of a casino in Biloxi, Mississippi.

Damaged Interstate 90 in Biloxi, Mississippi.

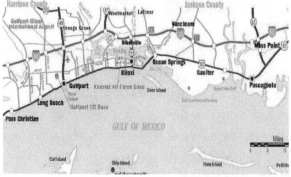

Postcards of the Mississippi Gulf Shoreline.

Second, it is important to remember that Mississippians received a twenty-four-hour evacuation notice from the Governor because the storm changed directions. Shortly thereafter, the powerful hurricane pummeled the Mississippi Gulf Coast region. The twenty-six-mile Gulf Coast infrastructure was ripped to pieces by the hurricane's force, leaving businesses, homes, and neighborhoods in shambles. As already mentioned, the estimated damage was over $100 billion. Immediately after the storm, this left residents strapped without access to roads, electricity, plumbing, or the ability to get basic necessities such as food and water. For these reasons and many others, the women saw the help they received and what was given to their community after the disaster as rays of light sent from God.

Three quarters of these Mississippi women said that the support they received from members of their local community immediately after the disaster was very beneficial. All of these women survivors mentioned a neighbor, friend, or family member who showed personal concern for them after the storm. Likewise, many women assisted friends by cooking, cleaning away debris, and bringing necessities for elderly neighbors who could not stand in long lines. While waiting for a week for outside help after the hurricane, several women said connecting with people in their community to support each other was helpful after Hurricane Katrina. This line of reasoning speaks to collectivism, a core principle of Womanism, which is made clear in the women's narratives later in this chapter.

Almost all of these Mississippi women survivors mentioned religion in several contexts during the interviews, so this theme was very important to them. Since Mississippi is located in the Bible Belt, it was not a surprise that God or faith played a significant role in grounding the women and helped them accept and manage the aftermath of Katrina's fury. Although religious beliefs were not the focus of Petry's (1944) book, in *Country Place*, faith was highlighted and mirrors the perspective of these Mississippi women's framework. For example, Petry's characters described damage to the church—a focal point of the city—feeling thankful to be alive, and saying a prayer during the hurricane. Likewise, these women survivors' faith correlates with the spiritual tenet of Womanist orientation. Some women spoke of how churches assisted them after the storm and others give specific examples of how they helped members of their community after Katrina, as their narratives will demonstrate in this chapter.

Another helpful resource these women survivors of Katrina mentioned were the volunteers, both secular and from faith-based organizations. All of these women saluted the volunteers' valiant efforts to support them personally—and their commitment to help them begin the rebuilding process. When speaking of community assistance, some women mentioned the state and federal government's response in Mississippi. Most of the women viewed the process as seamless. They attributed this to the fact that the state's Republican governor, Haley Barbour, had been a Washington insider before taking the post. Over half the women applied for and received the government's $2,000 relief stipend for people who survived Hurricane Katrina. Only one woman said she had problems with FEMA and did not get assistance until January 2006 (five months after the hurricane). She and her husband were turned down a number of times but were finally awarded a FEMA trailer because their home was destroyed by the hurricane. Several women said they did not need FEMA's assistance because of their ability to provide for themselves immediately after the storm, although they had damage to their home that was covered by their insurance company. The next section empowers these women disaster survivors to speak via their personal narratives as they describe what was helpful to them in their own words.

Betty, Gulfport, Mississippi
Just having something to do helped me a lot [after Hurricane Katrina]. I think God left a remnant of people here so that

we could be here to be caretakers of others—I really believe that. See, our church was not damaged [from Hurricane Katrina]. It was perfectly fine, but our sister churches in Pass Christian and Biloxi were destroyed. [Gulfport is between Pass Christian and Biloxi.] Therefore, our church became a place to help other people get back on their feet, and that gave me something to do. It made me feel like okay, I have a reason to be here. That helped me until we went back on the air. Another thing that helped me [after Hurricane Katrina] was about three or four weeks on the air [as a radio employee] and after listening to so many stories of the people in the area, I remember one of the ladies at the station saying to me, "Betty, you need to take advantage of this opportunity." You see, a hotel in Florida offered free weekend stays if you lived in an area that Katrina devastated. That's when she told me, "I have made reservations for you so you can get away from here for a weekend." I went, and it really helped me wind down and relax. You see, there was not one street on the entire Mississippi Gulf Coast where you could not see the devastation. There were no McDonalds, no movie theaters or restaurants. Going to Florida made me think about how beautiful the Coast was before Hurricane Katrina, and the trip gave me a new perspective since I am an ocean person. I started to see the end of the tunnel and felt much better about things. When I got back, I remember someone saying how strong I was. [Laughingly, Betty said,] For the first time I thought if one more person tells me how strong I am, I will knock them out! [Betty laughed out loud.] I didn't want to have to be strong anymore, but I was for myself and family. Really, in a way, I guess for the whole community. I remember after Katrina, people forgot about themselves and helped one another. You know, you just did what you did. I remember a lady down the street saying, "Listen, I got a freezer full of meat and it's going to spoil then I am going to have to throw it away. Do you know anybody who needs food?" I remember finding people for her to give the food to. I remember cooking food and giving it away. People helped each other cut down trees, cook, and clean up. That's what we are supposed to do. You know, I met really good people too. Like Jean, I met her somewhere trying to fight for things for people. I met a lot of wonderful people after Hurricane Katrina. [Betty's voice was filled with happiness when she made this comment.]

Laura, Gulfport, Mississippi
My family, friends, and the churches have helped me personally get through Katrina and start to rebuild my life. See, a few days after the storm, the lines to get basic necessities were so[ooo] long! [Laura held the word "so" for an extended time to emphasize the wait.] I remember a group called the North Carolina Men. They came and stayed until the end of the year [2005]. They had a system that worked really well. They had a drive-thru right after the storm to get the basics like ice, water, and hot food. [Katrina hit at the end of the summer when temperatures were 100°F.] The North Carolina Men just asked you what you needed and how much; then they put it in the trunk of your car. That kept the line moving. It was very efficient and helpful, especially when people were already so stressed out right after the storm. One very helpful person was my next-door neighbor, a white man. We had a speaking and friendly relationship before Katrina. See, he had a working water well on his property, and he provided water for our street to flush the toilets every evening until the utility company turned the water back on. The water was truly a blessing to all of us on my street. Of course, [Laura said with a smile on her face]

we all know each other much better now. Katrina brought people closer together. When I was out, I would pick up ice, water, and food for the older people on my street. All of us looked out for each other. Another helpful thing after Katrina was the church. People came from out of town to help us. I will never forget the people who came from across the country to help people clean the debris away and salvage what they could. The college students came too. They had the energy to help people clean up their yards and homes. [Laura added,] My faith kept me during and after Katrina. (You have to remember, my son and I were in this house during the storm.) We prayed and I know God was with us. I know that's the reason we are still here.

Corene, Gulfport, Mississippi

If it had not been for the church groups [from] other states who came to help us, some people would still not be in their houses today. It was because of the faith-based organizations that a lot of us are back in our homes. It is because of the young people who took spring breaks, Christmas breaks, summer breaks, and those who are still coming to the Mississippi Gulf Coast to help us. These kids will stay in [any type of] shelter just to help us. The faith-based groups [stayed] in shelters too. A few stayed in mobile homes that were available. They came anyway [regardless of the living conditions that were available after the storm]. Some even brought materials to help us. So we will never forget that and not just in Gulfport, I'm talking about from Waveland [the most western Mississippi city which borders Louisiana] all the way to the Mobile [Alabama] line [the most eastern Mississippi city]. Another thing that helped, and even surprised me, was how people who survived Katrina themselves, who had lost their homes, were so generous with their last possessions, even food and water. People were so generous and everyone shared, and believe me, [Corene said emphatically,] at that time there was very little to share, but everybody shared what they had. The way my neighbors came together after the storm was wonderful. Neighbors came to your house just to see if you were okay or if you needed anything. The compassion I saw after Katrina was the most helpful thing of all. That helped my spirit survive Katrina. It really did.

Sam, Pass Christian, Mississippi
The biggest thing that has gotten me through since Katrina has been my faith. It has been strengthened for sure. Also, the love that was shown by so many people outside our community who came to help us was overwhelming. That was a blessing! Two, I developed new relationships with people outside of our area, and I'm still keeping in contact with some of those individuals. As a result of all of the help that we got after Katrina, we rebuilt our church and decided to form a disaster relief group. So when Texas got hit by Hurricane Ike [2009], our church group went down to help those survivors. I re-evaluated what's important and what's not important, like making six figures. Yes, you need money to live, but that can't be everything. I'm thankful for my family and community. I have reassessed everything, and I think my entire family has too. It was tough right after Katrina. See, we were in small quarters and we didn't have TV, so we had to talk and communicate more. We just had good, clean fun. I learned in a new way that it's okay to be dependent on people. You see, I am an independent type of person. But I realized that I can ask for help with things and just let that pride go. I have always thought and believed as other people thought—if my grandmother and mother could

do what they had to do, surely, I can do this too! [Sam stated matter-of-factly,] I come from a strong line of women. I'm thankful to be a survivor, really an overcomer, and for the assistance we got after Katrina.

Ellen, Biloxi, Mississippi

My Christian friends really helped me after Katrina. My faith in God is stronger. God provided all my needs. It was God, my family, and friends who supported me after the storm. My job provided a place for me and my husband to live in one of the dormitories because FEMA said we were not eligible for assistance because we had flood insurance and owned our home, but it was gone and we didn't have anywhere to live. That was very helpful after the hurricane. [Ellen said this slowly and in a very sad tone.] We were never sure of why our FEMA case was closed three times before we were given a trailer five months after the storm, but it eventually worked out. My family came to help me get my life together as best as I could. People from out of state helped us too. The volunteers have been very helpful and supportive to me and our community. They helped us gut out the rubbish from our home and salvage a few things to keep as memories from our house. It seems to me that the nation was closer right after Katrina, at least in Mississippi.

Helen, Gulfport, Mississippi

One thing that was most helpful for me after Katrina was having flood and home insurance. I had minor damage on my home, and my insurance company paid me above the allocation on my home and for damages. I had some other problems with my insurance company, but overall my experience was positive. But not losing my house like so many people did made me feel guilty. It's hard to explain.

[The feeling Helen described is commonly known as survivor's guilt (Nader, 1990).] The government and friends were helpful to me, but my family was not on the Coast to help. I helped other people after the storm, and that was a great feeling. Overall, the experience of Hurricane Katrina has changed me forever. I don't want everything right now anymore, but I want a back-up plan in case anything like this happens again.

Joanne, Gulfport, Mississippi

I didn't lose very much and didn't need FEMA's assistance because before Katrina, I had a really good job and had savings, but my family and friends did need FEMA's help. [Joanne was one of the women who chose not to go back to her management position after Katrina.] Everyone pulled together to help each other. I provided shelter for a friend who had no place to stay so he could get back on his feet. My insurance came through for me and the response time was quick, within two weeks after the storm. But my first conversations with my insurance company were irritating. They kept looking for watermarks, but I didn't have any watermarks. I just had roof and wind damage. But, in the end, it all worked out. After Katrina, [Joanne sighed deeply and said, "Give me just a minute,"] I have seen people show true love for others from all across the world by volunteering to help us. Our neighbors, even if they never really spoke before, now everyone checks on everyone else. Humankind can be kind to each other. Thank you for helping us too. It's important that people like yourself continue to get the word out that we are still here. Thank you for not forgetting us.

Over half of the women in this study echoed Joanne's feelings that after Hurricane Katrina, Mississippi had been overlooked.

The volunteers' presence communicated to these Mississippi Black women survivors immediately after the disaster and over the years that they had not been forgotten. In some ways, these visible helpers provided rays of hope. Their presence helped these women continue to stay focused and believe that life would get better as they helped their friends and family members continue the process of rebuilding their lives, homes, and communities after the hurricane. The women continue to discuss what was helpful after the disaster.

Jean, Biloxi, Mississippi
The volunteers were the ones who saved us. If it had not been for them, we would not be as far along as we are. Some came and stayed. Others kept coming back because of the relationships we have built with them. They helped the seniors and the single parents get their houses gutted out. The volunteers have come through in ways you can't imagine. See, when you know Mr. Bill and Ms. Mary, it makes a difference. See, building relationships matter so much and this was only possible because the volunteers kept coming back. Another thing was meeting people who I could talk to about real problems. I liked discussing how to go about solving them and how to do the right thing not in a judging way, but in a helpful way. It was good to know that friends were still alive and to know that they had survived that monstrous hurricane. Really, it was just good to be able to talk to people and get things done that needed to be done because, you know, people don't think about Mississippi when they think of Katrina. People outside of the region didn't even think Mississippi was affected by Katrina. Boy, were they wrong. Our infrastructure on the Coast was wiped out in several cities, and even though the volunteers have helped us tremendously, we still have a lot more to do. Insurance companies, they want to collect money, but

they don't want to give it back to you when you need help. Eventually, I got paid, but it wasn't because they really wanted to help me after the storm, that's for sure. [Jean chuckled softly, then said,] Even Trent Lott had problems with the insurance company at first. [Trent Lott was Mississippi's senior senator at the time. After Katrina, he filed a lawsuit because he had trouble settling his claim against a major insurance company after Katrina demolished his Victorian Oceanfront vacation home in Gulfport.]

Jean's comments on insurance companies, like Joanne's statement, are representative of another sub-theme from the data analysis. Over half of these women described their first conversations with insurance companies as frustrating, but they were satisfied with the settlements they received in the end. Some women said the insurance company's assessment and payment was as short as two weeks or within a few months after Katrina. Only one of these women had to wait over a year for compensation because of her condominium association's negotiation process.

Catherine, Pass Christian, Mississippi
Six weeks after I lost my home on the beach, my business, and everything else, the ministry [her church] called me and asked me to come to work at the Compassion Center. I was doing what I loved to do. I had a safe place to live. All of my needs were met spiritually, physically, socially, and emotionally. For that time, it was, in a strange way, almost better than it was before Katrina. It was just the awesomeness of God and how He provides. I have been royally provided for. I had nothing after Katrina; prior to the storm, I had plenty. Since the disaster, I have been able to do everything that I want to do. I exercised, I ate right, I went to conferences, mostly spiritual to help me get back

on track. It's not like sitting in a parched office, not looking at the beach, but God provided, he provided manna from heaven for me. [Catherine lowered her voice, not sadly, but in a way that indicated acceptance.] Looking to the future, I'm not sure of what will happen, but I believe that God is going to do it for me again.

Jeanette, Pass Christian, Mississippi

My family was really helpful to me after Katrina. To talk to them on the phone and know that they were so happy I was safe meant so much to me and Joe [Jeanette's husband]. I knew that I was loved before the storm, but after Katrina, I saw it in a different way because of the love of so many people. See, right after Katrina we didn't have cell phone service, but when our phones were turned back on we had calls from New York, California, Arizona, and Texas in our voicemail box. My old New York church family was very supportive—just having that support even from afar was very helpful. They did not forget about Joe and me. They would call my mother if they couldn't reach me to check on us, and that really meant a lot to us—not being forgotten. Another thing that was helpful was my relationship with my husband. We never had a lot of problems or issues [in our relationship], there is a significant age difference between us, but like most couples we have our things come up from time to time. Both of us happen to be very resilient people. We had gone through different things in life before we met each other. We have gone through experiences together. We have many moments where I complete his sentences and he completes mine. We just have that kind of connection and that helped us as a couple. Granted, there have been separations, divorces, and crises since Katrina because they tend to bring out or spotlight problems, but I believe because we knew who we were going into it, we were going to be Jeanette and Joe throughout it and at the end of it. We continued to talk to each other [she said with emphasis]. He, the very, very patient man, put up with my irritability. I dealt with his moments too. It's not often but at times you have to give them a little love too [she said, smiling]. He's been a strong force, and he went back to work so that I could continue the process of getting my Masters. [Jeanette completed her Masters of Divinity degree.] I credit school as the third helpful thing after Katrina because it gave me something to do. My relationship with God has improved too. God sustained me and us through Katrina. Looking back, it's interesting that my mom made an observation after reading my diary. [Jeanette kept a diary of what happened to her after Katrina.] My mom said that I was irritable and angry at one point, but on the outside I didn't act that out, I just told everyone that everything's going to be okay, we're fine, we're healthy, and we're good, but on the inside I was angry and irritable all the time. My mom said I appeared to move on sometime later. It took me some time to manage those feelings and get through everything. She thinks my movement was like going through the stages of grief. Another thing, I have built many new relationships since the storm and my faith was strengthened because of Hurricane Katrina. I let pride go! [Jeanette said emphatically.] See, Katrina taught me a lot about what I need and what I don't need. It made a big impact on my life. I'm full circle.

Jeanette's narrative provides a window to understand the ways in which these women managed their emotions and remained stable after Katrina so that readers can view all aspects of these women's lives. Whenever one of the women talked about how she felt immediately after the storm, each described the pain in several ways.

Some said Katrina was so bad, while others briefly lowered their head or paused to compose themselves. As the interviews continued, these women moved from a distraught mood to a purposeful resolve to overcome Katrina. Some women said their faith helped them cope; others said helping members of their community made them feel good and was therapeutic. Sam said, "If my grandmother and mother could do what they had to do, surely I can do this too. See, I came from a strong line of women." Another woman, Betty, said, "I think God left a remnant of people here to be strong and help other people get back on their feet." These women's ability to experience and manage one of the worst disasters in American history and still move forward is a testament of their determination, stamina, and chutzpah which are all Womanist's tenets. Despite the force of Katrina and its emotional upheaval, these women remained sturdy after the storm for themselves, their families, and their communities to begin the process of rebuilding their lives.

Another aspect of Jeanette's account reveals how her relationship with her husband improved after Katrina. This was the case with three other women in this study, Betty, Sam, and Ellen. Betty and her male friend, who weathered the storm together with her aging father in Gulfport, eventually decided to get married after Katrina. Sam, who was divorced, reconnected and married a former high school friend. Ellen and her husband recently celebrated their Ruby (40th) wedding anniversary. Although each of these women acknowledged that the storm added stressors for them and their families, it strengthened their relationships with their mates. Note: one woman (Lynne) and her husband were in the process of divorce prior to Katrina, but they stayed together for several months after the storm for the sake of their two children. They finalized the divorce process one year after the storm.

Mary, Gulfport, Mississippi
After Katrina, there was a lady from my church, Ms.

Dickerson, I saw her at the grocery store one day and she asked me, what needs to happen to keep you here on the Gulf Coast? I told her I needed a job. As soon as I said that, she just started to pray with me right in the grocery store. When she finished she told me, God is able and God is faithful. She said that I needed to believe that this was going to happen. Really, that meant so much to me. It was really what I needed at the time because I was feeling discouraged. As time passed, things started to turn around for me. [Mary got a job with FEMA a little later and is still working there today.]

Like almost all of the women in this study, Mary's description of how her faith played a dynamic role in helping her cope after Katrina, as well as the assistance of people in her neighborhood, speaks volumes about the ways in which these women survivors lived daily after Katrina. Likewise, the women's spirituality and collectivism are focal points of Womanism. These women saw God's role and provision for them before, during, and after Katrina as a reality in their lives. Almost all of these women referred to their church, God, or their faith. Some of the women referred to the faith-based volunteers as "blessings." Their faith-based lifestyles might be dismissed because of Mississippi's proximity in the Bible Belt, but it was evident that regardless of how they are perceived, surviving Katrina was, without a doubt, for them and their communities, connected to their faith in God and rebuilding their lives.

In conclusion, this chapter highlighted the key factors that these Mississippi Black women survivors of Hurricane Katrina said were most helpful to them after the disaster. The hurricane destroyed the Gulf Coast's infrastructure and devastated the way of life of citizens in the region. It is remarkable that there were survivors of the catastrophe and only 238 deaths (Biloxi Memorial, 2015) in Mississippi. One salient finding from almost all of the women in this study was that their faith in God helped them deal with the aftermath of the disaster after the loss of their homes, possessions, and in some cases jobs. These women said that their faith was strengthened after Katrina because, in their view, God provided for them even in the barren place in which they found themselves after the storm. The women's proclamation of faith speaks to their Womanist standpoint. In fact, after Katrina, some of these women said that they believed it was God's will that they assist others inside and outside of their community.

Much has been written about Hurricane Katrina survivors and FEMA. Interestingly, the women in this study had very little to say about their experience with FEMA. Three-fourths of these Mississippi Black Katrina survivors reported applying for and receiving assistance from the federal government. Most of the women who applied for the $2,000 FEMA disaster relief award, after the hurricane, said that it was a seamless process. Several women said that they did not need FEMA's assistance because of their ability to provide for themselves immediately after the storm even though they had damage to their homes. These women were married and said that they had money in savings accounts that they could use to handle unexpected emergencies like the storm. Several other women said that they had access to community resources and information because of their personal networks.

Another striking finding was that all of the women mentioned the valiant efforts of the church-based organizations, students, and volunteers who came to help Hurricane Katrina survivors after the disaster. These Mississippi women expressed gratitude that the volunteers took the time to help them rebuild their communities after Katrina. One woman said, "The North Carolina men's group provided hot food, water, and ice, in 100°F temperatures, which was extremely important immediately after the disaster since Katrina hit at the end of a hot summer." Likewise, three women stated emphatically that the "church volunteers saved them." Other women said that "they couldn't have rebuilt their homes or communities" as fast as they did without the help of the faith-based organization volunteers. These Mississippi women championed the student volunteers who came from across the country and had the energy to do what was needed to assist the survivors as the rebuilding of the community moved forward over the years. What's more, the volunteers' efforts had such an impact that one woman's church formed its own disaster relief volunteer group to assist those in the affected area less fortunate than themselves.

The third salient factor that helped these women after Katrina was friends and neighbors from their local community. Many women said that friends, family members, and neighbors gave them basic supplies and vital information immediately after the hurricane. One woman said, "A neighbor supplied the people on her street with water from his well to flush their toilets, which was a luxury after Katrina" because the utilities were not operational for over a week after the storm. Several women expressed their appreciation for people from their local communities who came to their homes just to check on them and to see if they needed anything like water or ice, a scarcity in those neighborhoods that were without electricity for weeks after Katrina.

Finally, a meaningful finding that contributes to the disaster canon in regard to Black women survivors in particular is that over half of these women said that they met new people after the disaster and formed new long-term personal friendships that did not exist before the storm. This discovery speaks to the Womanist principle of collectivity. Traditionally, Black women have developed kinships, but it is significant that even in the case of a life-threatening natural disaster, like Hurricane Katrina, Black women reached beyond themselves and formed new bonds that sustained both themselves and members of their community when resources were scarce. One woman attributed her new profession as CEO of an organization to the people she met after Katrina. Another said she has new and dear friends whom she met while standing in long lines for hours after the storm. Since these women met under dire circumstances, it is reasonable to think that they bonded after the disaster and viewed widening their social circle as a benefit to themselves and others. This chapter discussed the factors these Mississippi women survivors said were most helpful to them after Hurricane Katrina to start the rebuilding process. The next chapter will discuss the women's lives a decade after the storm, in 2015.

CHAPTER 7
AFTER A DECADE: WHERE ARE THE WOMEN AND HOW ARE THEY DOING?

SINCE THE 2005 STORM, the process of recovery has been slow but steady for citizens on the Gulf Coast. These Mississippi women worked through the chaos after Katrina and have made substantial progress from the tattered lives they were left with after the disaster. What's more, these women remain determined to move forward resiliently, to regain the middle-class lifestyle they were accustomed to before the hurricane. This chapter will allow these Mississippi Black women survivors to talk about what has changed in their lives since 2005 when the storm devastated the Gulf Coast. The women will discuss many topics—and changes they have made since the storm. Some common themes of recovery include new evacuation plans, remodeling or rebuilding of their homes, and personal changes in their life perspective. In addition, some women will highlight individual changes, such as new marriages, educational attainment, and how they have introduced leisure into their lives again.

Prior to Hurricane Katrina, some of the women described their evacuation plan in a "pick up and go" fashion. But since the disaster, almost all of these Mississippi Black women said that they have developed a definitive evacuation plan, which includes routes and locations of where they will go. In addition, these women said they had discussed their evacuation plan with their family and some friends. Each woman will discuss their updated evacuation plan in depth in this chapter. After Hurricane Katrina, three-fourths of these Mississippi women survivors had damage to their homes and several of their homes were destroyed. Despite that, ten years later, all of these women have managed the process and rebuilt, remodeled, or bought new homes. The women will discuss the navigation of this monumental feat and where they are today in the personal narrative section later in the chapter.

As was mentioned in Chapter 6, Hurricane Katrina brought a screeching halt to employment opportunities for the Mississippi Gulf Coast's citizenry in just one day. Unemployment in the region rose exponentially, reaching an astounding 24.3 percent in October 2005 (US Department of Labor, 2015; BLS, 2006). After the catastrophe, all of these women except one lost her job. In the face of little to no hope, all the women found new jobs as discussed in the previous chapter. Most of them have changed jobs several times since the hurricane. The women will describe their current position and how they view their careers ten years after the disaster. In addition to managing the dilemma of rebuilding and finding employment after Katrina, some of these women set goals and had personal accomplishments. These actions are both commendable and remarkable. For example, several of these Mississippi Black women earned graduate degrees and others found life partners after 2005. Each woman will highlight aspects of their achievements in this chapter's narrative section.

Lastly, most of these women said that they had made and found a time to enjoy life again. One woman said it best when she noted that finding time to relax is important "just to stay balanced." These women continue the process of recovery by recreating the lifestyles they had before the hurricane. Womanist scholar Layli Phillips Maparyan (2006) refers to actions like these as non-ideological or fluid, even innate, characteristics. Educator Nannie Burroughs said emphatically that, "Black women do the 'wholly impossible.'"

Historian, Darlene Clark Hines' (1995) book, whose title honors Burroughs', provides a plethora of examples that highlight the types of heroic actions these Mississippi Black women Hurricane Katrina survivors demonstrated. Narrative theory will allow the women to provide concrete examples of their Womanist characteristics in their own words, such as the value of their faith, their desire to stay connected to their community and family members. The time has come for these Mississippi Black women to describe where they are—and how their recovery is progressing—ten years since Hurricane Katrina's devastating blow to the Gulf Coast.

Catherine, Pass Christian, Mississippi

I'm doing okay today. Remember, before Katrina I had a beachfront home in Pass Christian. Now I live in a gated community in the Back Bay neighborhood [in Gulfport, where property value in that part of town is regionally pricey]. My new condo is still very close to the water [Catherine said proudly]. After Katrina, I used some of my insurance money to buy this place and some to travel. Looking back on it now, that may not have been the wisest choice, but it was what I wanted and needed to do for myself at that time. My trip to Israel was a personal spiritual growth journey. It gave me perspective, and I felt like it was a new start [for me] after Katrina. It also brought me even closer to God than I already was.

As far as my career is concerned, I had built a thriving social work practice in the area before the hurricane, and I am slowly, but surely, rebuilding my practice. It's not as big as it was before the storm, but I'm happy with it at this point. See, I decided to go back to school to finish my Doctorate degree, which I had started before Katrina. It was a good feeling to get that completed! I know having my Doctorate will help me expand the business further in time. See, I am a certified trauma therapist now. [Catherine is also a licensed social worker.]

For fun, I spend time with my grandchildren. I have three [grandchildren] now. They are ten, eight, and six years old. I spend every minute of my leisure time with them. I'm with them on holidays, birthdays, at school events, and almost everything else [that] they do. They bring me joy! Being with them makes me forget all about Katrina. That's why if there is another serious disaster threat, my family knows I am evacuating to where they are in Atlanta.

Sam, Pass Christian, Mississippi
I am doing very well. After Katrina, my company offered me the opportunity to transfer to another region. You see, I was the human resource manager for the largest casino on the coast [Sam stated proudly], but I chose not to do that. See, after the storm, I re-evaluated everything in my life, and making six figures was not that important to me anymore. I accepted a position as the human resources director for a city on the coast and have been in that job ever since. I know and like my job and plan to stay there until I retire in a few years [Sam said, smiling].

After Katrina, my house had twelve feet of water, so I lost everything inside [of it]. But the foundation and frame of my house withstood the storm, and I remodeled [it]. Of course, having insurance made that process much easier. I built a new deck off the kitchen, which was what I always wanted [to do] but didn't have [done] before Katrina. I am enjoying my old, no, new home! [Sam said excitedly.]

Another thing that has happened since the storm, well, I

started dating a man after Katrina, and we are now married. [Sam smiled splendidly.] My life is full, and I am happy. My sons, their wives and children are here all the time. One of my sons and his family live right next door, and the other son's family has moved back to the Coast. We spend lots of time together. My husband's children visit too. I love spending time with my grandchildren and niece. I have invested a lot in them, and they are all doing well in school. Sometimes we take vacations together, and that brings us closer together as a family. See, since Katrina, I realized just how important my family is, not money. I am also very active in my church. I am busy coordinating the Gone Fishing Ministry that started through my church. It is now a 501c program. We offer disaster relief to people who need it.

When I asked Sam whether or not she had an evacuation plan, she said:

Oh, absolutely, I do [have an evacuation plan]. See, before Katrina, since I was essential personnel at my job, our plan was staggered. My family would go to Birmingham or Montgomery [Alabama], and I would go to the location my job had for us. We've used this plan seventy-two hours before every storm in the past. But, since Katrina, we have discussed our evacuation plan. We would never wait around like we did with Katrina for a job or anything. My brother kept on saying, you see, I'm the youngest of four [children], we need to do a telephone tree in case something happens and none of us have cell phones that work. You see, after Katrina cell phones didn't work for a day or two. So we [my family] decided we would use our cousin who lives in Shreveport as our point of contact for everyone if we can't get in touch with each other. Hopefully, we will never need this evacuation plan, but if we do, we have it.

Betty, Gulfport, Mississippi

Well, I guess the best way to put it is I'm doing okay. See, I lost my dad [after Katrina]. He had Alzheimer's, and I was his primary caregiver until he died. [Before Katrina, Betty, her husband, and her dad weathered the storm because her father refused to leave.] That has been hard on me, but I'm doing okay. My brother and his wife live next door, and it's good to have them close, but I miss my dad. My husband has been very supportive. [Prior to Katrina, Betty had reunited with her high school sweetheart after forty years, and now they are married.] We have known each other for a long time, so I am blessed to have him in my life. He [her husband] knew my dad well since we have known each other since high school. [Betty is one of two women in the study who was single and got married after the hurricane.]

Before Katrina, I worked as an on-air radio personality at Gulfport's urban station for over ten years, but I decided it was time for a change. So, in 2006, I decided to use my [college] degree to get a job in the school system. Now, I coordinate a mentoring and tutorial program for students who need extra help and support. The program provides after-school support each day. The job change has been rewarding, and it keeps me busy. I have to find the mentors and organize all of the tutorial sessions at multiple schools. It's a never-ending process, but the program really helps the kids and that's what really matters.

In regard to my home, [you might] remember we stayed here in my dad's home because he refused to leave. The home that I purchased is next door to his [home]. We did not have a lot of damage from Hurricane Katrina; we were really blessed. We had insurance and have completed all of the home repairs from Katrina's damage. I plan to stay in this house until I retire. Since this house survived Camille and Katrina, I know I will be safe [Betty said, smiling], because I can't imagine a storm being any worse than Katrina. [Betty's expression changed to a very serious gaze.] But if there is another serious threat of a hurricane, my siblings and I will evacuate for sure. [Betty chuckled when she told me about her evacuation plan.] Although I've lived on the coast all my life, we really didn't have a plan because our home, that my dad built, survived Camille in '69 and now Katrina. Before my dad died, my husband said, if another storm comes, [Betty paused and laughed out loud] we are medicating your daddy and taking him wherever we go because we are not going through that [type of] craziness again. [Betty's father was over eighty years old. He died in 2013.] We have talked about where we will go, and my family talks about storms much more often now than we ever did. You know, it depends on where the storm is coming from whether we would go to Little Rock [Arkansas] or somewhere else. We've even talked about evacuating to see family in New York, Kansas City, or Mobile. We know we have to get a head start now. Before my dad died, my sister and I discussed that we might have to put him on a plane and fly him to Little Rock in case we get another storm threat like Katrina. We have discussions about evacuation options now on a regular basis. [She said this with a smile on her face.]

Jeanette, Pass Christian, Mississippi
I am doing well. When Katrina hit, I was in the process of completing my Masters of Divinity [MDiv] degree. The aftermath of the storm briefly interrupted my studies, but I finished my MDiv in 2009. Thank God. It was a lot of work, but having it has made a big difference in my life. Right after

Katrina, I started looking for work but could not find a job, so my mother said, Jeanette, maybe all you are supposed to do right now is go to school. Although it didn't make sense that I couldn't get a job, my husband was supportive and took an extra job so that I could focus on school and finish, which I did. Today, I am the pastor of two Methodist churches on the Coast. My congregations are small, but they keep me busy and productive. I am happy I finished my MDiv because I feel I am doing what I am supposed to be doing right now and where I am supposed to be at this time. Last year, I was nominated and chosen as one of *Parade* magazine's featured persons in their annual issue of the incomes of professionals and how much money people make in America. That was a pleasant surprise and honor. [Jeanette smiled broadly.] As far as our house is concerned, Joe [Jeanette's husband] and I came to an agreement with our insurance company within a month after Katrina. We were very fortunate. So we were able to start the cleaning, repairing, and remodeling process of our damaged home, which had water damage and over five feet of mud inside. We still own and live in our home today. Fortunately, [Jeanette smiled] I have an apartment that is provided by the denomination, which is between the two churches that I pastor, so I don't have to take the hour-long drive back and forth to home each day on Interstate 90. Sometimes, it serves as a getaway spot for Joe and I. We have also gone on a cruise and are planning to take another one next year—just to relax. My denomination has also sent me to a few conferences that were out of state. Although it is work, we had some down time there too.

Jeanette's response to my questions about having an evacuation plan is as follows:

Oh yes! My husband and I have talked about where we will go on more than one occasion. We will evacuate for sure. Since I pastor two churches, I have talked to my Boards about an evacuation plan for each church. Today, all of our members at both churches know the plan and timeline.

Corene, Gulfport, Mississippi
I am doing very well. Since Katrina, I have retired from [my] political seat in Jackson [capital of Mississippi]. Katrina was very exhausting for all of us here on the Coast. It was a monster storm, much worse than Camille. It damaged a lot of property, and a lot of people lost their jobs. As for me, I didn't have a lot of damage and the little bit that I had was repaired right after the storm. My insurance paid my claim immediately. I had no problems, but I know a lot of people who did. Since I retired, I have had time to spend even more time with my grand- and great-grandchildren, which I enjoy dearly.

Regarding her evacuation plan, Corene said:

Yes, we had an evacuation plan, but my son worked for the Isle of Capri [a large casino in Biloxi], and they had to close down and make sure everything was ready for the hurricane. We waited on him, so we didn't leave until the day before the hurricane. We went to Florida. It was the first time in my life I've ever gone towards Florida during a hurricane. I usually go up towards Jackson [Mississippi] or Memphis [Tennessee]. But we went to Florida and waited [for] the hurricane [to pass]. Before Katrina we didn't talk about evacuating from hurricanes, but we knew we would leave. See, I remember Camille [1969 hurricane]. Since Katrina, we have talked about it a lot more, and what I think we have all come up with is when they tell us [a hurricane] is off the coast of Africa, we're going to be looking for a place to go. [Corene laughed as she made this statement.] I think one of the things Katrina taught us was [that] there are no material things that are worth your life. Nothing has the value you thought it did, and things you thought you couldn't live without—Katrina taught us how to live without them. So I think mostly what we think about now is how to get out of here as soon as possible. Yes, we definitely have a plan to evacuate [Corene said frankly].

Laura, Gulfport, Mississippi
I'm okay, I won't complain. See, since Katrina, my main goal has been to remain employed full-time, and I have done that. See, I am single. That means I am responsible and have maintained all that I have acquired over the last forty years. My two sons are grown, and I want to take care of things for as long as I can on my own. I had extensive damage to my house since a part of my roof collapsed in my master bedroom. That caused water damage in over half of my house. I had to have a lot of work done on my house. I have remodeled and refurnished two bedrooms, two baths, and my kitchen since Katrina, and stainless steel kitchens are not cheap [Laura said, smiling]. I didn't have any problems with my insurance, so that process went smoothly, but I had to live in my house while it was being renovated. If you have ever had major work done in a home, you know that's a headache. But I am happy with the way my house looks now! [Laura smiled broadly.] I am satisfied with it and enjoy the time I have to spend here after work and on the weekends. I am most proud of the fact that regardless of how difficult the economy has been since Katrina, although I have changed jobs three times and may have to change again, I have been employed full-

time. That is a blessing, and I thank God for providing for me. I have even been able to take a few leisure out-of-town trips with my friends and family. I have supported a friend's formal events [which] gave me an opportunity to dress up and have fun. [Laura smiled gently.]

Laura had this to say about her disaster plan:

Yes, I have a tentative plan. It's sort of like the plan I had before Katrina, which was to evacuate even though I didn't do that because I was waiting for my son [Laura's son had to work, and when he arrived, the weather was too bad for them to leave so they rode out Katrina in her home, which lost a part of the roof during the hurricane], but he did not arrive early enough for us to evacuate. I have a couple of hotels that I have gathered information on where I can make reservations. My plan would be to leave as early as possible, make reservations, and go there to wait the storm out. You just have to be prepared. I have a credit card that I keep a zero balance on because I don't know how long I would have to be gone. See, a lot of time they [the authorities] won't let you back into the county. I have some cash set aside in case I have to leave. I have discussed the plan with family and friends since hurricane season starts again in June. I know if there is a threat of a hurricane, nine times out of ten, I'll probably leave especially since the terrible time we experienced during Katrina.

Helen, Gulfport, Mississippi
Well, I'm doing pretty good. I have changed the type of work that I do, but I still work for the federal government. Now my job sends me out to assist others who have survived disasters. I have worked in the Midwest, Texas, and New Jersey with Hurricane Sandy survivors. In many ways, Katrina has given

me a new career and an opportunity to travel. Although this is not a permanent job, it is somewhat stable to do because of the nature of disasters in the world. As far as my home is concerned, yes, it sustained some damage, but compared to other people's homes, my damage was not nearly as bad after Katrina. Since I had insurance, my settlement was within a month after the storm. Getting someone reliable to repair my damage was the challenge, but finally I found a good person to do the work. My home is my haven when I am not working. I am comfortably settled and relaxed here now.

Regarding a disaster plan, Helen said:

Prior to Katrina, I would just go home up Highway 49 [one of the main throughways from the Mississippi coast inland]. It usually takes about an hour and a half. Now since Katrina, of course, yes, I do [have an evacuation plan]. I will still take Highway 49, but I know another way to take through Poplarville [a town in the western central part of Mississippi] to get home. [Helen's home town is Meridian.] I would hit a lot of small towns like Purvis and Tylertown traveling on a lot of two-lane roads. I don't know all the roads, but I can get that information easy. I went that way once and it was actually quite nice. It was different. My brother and sister take that route all the time. We have talked about it a few times since Katrina. We talked about texting each other too. See, after Katrina most telephones were out and the only way you could contact people was through text. It would take a couple of minutes, sometimes a little longer, but at least I could receive and send text messages. We just texted each other and said where we were [located] and to say we are okay. We can't all go home because there are ten of us, so we know we'll be spread out and probably stay in hotels.

Ellen, Biloxi, Mississippi

I'm doing well. Remember, before Katrina I worked for a government agency as a manager after the storm. Since then, I have worked for a few other social service agencies. I like my job and enjoy helping students figure out what to do with their lives. I'm busy all the time. Since I lost everything except the frame and foundation of my house after Katrina, my husband and I had to start all over. We used our insurance payment to defray most of the personal expenses to build our new home on the same property. We love [Ellen held the word "love" a long time] our new home! [Ellen's new home is a four-bedroom two-story structure.] We have lived here for a few years now. My daughter teased me after our new home was built, she said, "Well, Mom, Katrina gave you a new house." [Ellen smiled softly as she spoke these words.] I am active in my sorority, and it has provided me with an outlet to have fun before and since Katrina. I have traveled to all of the regional and national conferences since I pledged, and I wouldn't let Katrina stop me from continuing that tradition. My husband and I have also gone on a cruise to vacation in St. Lucia since the hurricane.

In regard to developing a disaster plan since Hurricane Katrina, Ellen said:

Well, our plan has not changed. We have always just planned to leave when a bad hurricane comes to the Gulf Coast. I did not grow up here on the coast. So my plan was to get my pictures and leave. I don't really have a plan other than that [one]. I don't think I will ever stay here for a hurricane, especially since the area that I live in is a flood zone. Even though it was noted as an area that did not flood, that's what happened to my house. I got flood water. [Ellen lives in the Back Bay section of Biloxi, which was hit hard during Katrina—everything inside her home was destroyed.] I already know that if a hurricane is approaching, regardless of whether it is a category one, two, or three, I'm leaving. So that's my plan.

Mary, Gulfport, Mississippi
I am doing great! I worked for the same agency since Katrina, but I have switched positions. My new position required additional training so I had to take a lot of sessions online. I have completed all of them and now I travel all over the United States for the agency. Since I'm single, this is not an issue and it gives me a chance to see the country and help people. Since Katrina, I am most proud of the fact that I purchased a new three-bedroom ranch-style home in 2012. At my housewarming party, I received so many nice gifts from my friends who also survived Katina. It has really been nice to move into a place that is becoming my solace.

Mary said this to say about having a disaster plan:

I keep a bag packed. I keep my medicine handy, I keep water, a big supply of water on hand, and I keep my car full [of gas]. I have an alternative route other than Highway 49 to leave the coast to go home because I am from north Mississippi. Since I live alone, I have discussed it with my family in the northern part of the state. I told them which route I will take, where I'm going, and [that they should] give me [a certain amount of] time to call them. I have several people, friends and family, that I'm going to call to let them know that I am okay if we get another serious threat of a hurricane.

Hurricane Katrina decimated the Mississippi Gulf Coast in 2005, but the Black women survivors in this study have worked tirelessly to recover. This chapter enabled these resilient Mississippi women to share a part of their narratives on where they were ten years after the catastrophe. First, the women survivors discussed housing changes. Some of them live in the same home. All of their damaged homes have been remodeled. Others have purchased new homes. The participants' Womanist standpoint played a key role in their remarkable ability to recover, rebuild, and remain resolute to regain the middle-class lifestyles and the assets they had prior to Hurricane Katrina. Today, all of these women still live on the Mississippi Gulf Coast. The women's orientation or fluidity helped them balance their emotions and choose healthy options to manage the renovation and rebuilding process after Katrina.

Second, the women's spiritual proclivities informed their positive perspective. Despite Katrina's immediate and long-term aftermath, almost all of these women were optimistic that things would get better. They had hope when there was little to no hope. This is another Womanist attribute, which points to their spiritual grounding.

Thirdly, the women's employment status today is significantly different than it was immediately after the storm. In spite of the high unemployment rate immediately after Hurricane Katrina, these women managed the dilemma effectively. In fact, all of these women found new jobs within six months after the disaster and have remained employed in full-time positions since 2005. Each of these Mississippi Katrina women survivors said that the hurricane helped them realize that spending time with family and serving their community are very important. This speaks to these survivors' collectivist ideology—a core Womanist tenet. Lastly, the women highlighted personal successes or proud moments they have had since Katrina. Some women achieved goals, such as obtaining new graduate degrees, including one Doctorate. One woman received national recognition for her career success. Several women built new lives by deciding to get married. What's more, these Mississippi women survivors of Katrina found time to relax and enjoy life again, whether they are spending time at home or taking family vacations. In conclusion, the examples described in this chapter illustrate the recovery of these Mississippi Black women survivors of Hurricane Katrina. The chapter highlighted the women's fluidity, which was evident in their approach toward recovery and their re-established station in life ten years after Katrina. I argue that their Womanist orientation was the key reason they recovered. These women withstood the hurricane's fury and continue to move forward.

CHAPTER 8
TIME HAS PASSED, LIFE IS BETTER: CONCLUSION AND RECOMMENDATIONS

HURRICANE KATRINA CHANGED the way Americans think about—and will respond to—natural disasters forever. When this project started in October 2005, it was my way of assisting the disaster survivors. Shortly thereafter, I realized that the women in this longitudinal study had a unique and overlooked perspective. Their valuable lessons and narratives could inform policymakers, academics, people who may experience disasters, and anyone with an interest in how Black women have overcome adversity through the ages. This chapter will highlight how these Hurricane Katrina Mississippi Black women survivors are doing today then suggest several ways future researchers can initiate studies on Black disaster survivors, which serve as guiding principles that can save lives.

Over the years, the resilience of these women is a testament to their fortitude to keep going despite the worst possible scenario that one could imagine experiencing in life. Although some of them lost all their possessions after the disaster, they did not give up but persevered until life became better. These women rebuilt their lives, and their experiences provide missing and novel information to the ever-growing body of literature on Hurricane Katrina and natural disasters. In fact, this volume is the only single-group study of Mississippi women survivors over time. It provides readers and researchers with nascent epistemological data on the final stage of disaster studies, namely recovery and reconstruction, which is rarely studied. Womanism enabled me to show how these women rebuilt their lives after the devastation based on their heritage and cultural orientation. Narrative theory served as a framework and gave these women agency to speak in their own voices to share detailed aspects of their recovery. At the end of this chapter, the women will speak in their own voices on where they are ten years after Hurricane Katrina.

Future Research & Recommendations

As disasters continue to impact the lives of people, there will continue to be more work to do. First, more longitudinal disaster studies with women and minorities, whether Black, Latino, Asian, or Caucasian, need to be conducted. Additional studies on Blacks in social classes other than low-income survivors need to be initiated. Studying up sociologically is an approach that needs more attention in the disaster field and will, like this book, yield results about Blacks and other ethnic groups' resilience and ability to recover after catastrophes. Another important reason to study middle- and upper-class disaster survivors is to dispel the myth that all Blacks and other people of color are poor, which is what the media usually highlights during the chaotic aftermath of disasters.

Second, those who have made themselves gatekeepers must allow women and researchers of color to offer critiques and feedback on their findings so that the voices of disaster survivors of color are captured and authenticated by insiders so that the survivors' lived experiences can come forth without restraint. An example of this approach, although not a natural disaster study, is the recently published eighty-year-old volume *Barracoon* (2018), which was written by a renowned Black woman writer, Zora Neale Hurston. At the time Hurston wrote the volume, her approach was considered an unconventional methodology by the gatekeepers. It captured the lived experience of her subject—Cudjo, the last living former slave in America. Hurston's book, like this volume, utilizes narrative theory and provides a model for scholars to follow because it yields authentic findings that have received praise and is highly regarded today. In addition, disaster scholars need to include more students of color in their research cohorts and allow them the freedom to openly discuss and even challenge the conclusions that are drawn from findings. Likewise, senior scholars must allow students to write from their cultural perspective, such as Womanism, without the fear of reprisal from primary investigators or professors.

Scholars of color need to conduct studies on minority disaster survivors so that their lived experiences and voices are normalized. To date, there are only a small number of ethnic social scientists whose work is in disaster studies. This must change. One model new researchers might consider is the tradition established by the late Nobel laureate Toni Morrison, although she did not write about natural disasters. Her articles and books realistically capture the everyday experience of Blacks' existence in America. Although her work is fiction, Morrison's technique can be applied across cultures in disaster studies to factually describe survivors' stories. These suggestions are only a starting point for those who continue or plan to study ethnic minority survivors' lived experiences after disasters. After almost twenty years as a lecturer and a conspicuous consumer of scholarly findings, following the women in this study since 2005 has convinced me that participants' words are more powerful than any analysis of them. Said another way, analysis is bereft without prolific participant voices. So in the words of the late Maya Angelou, "when someone shows you who they are—believe them" and allow disaster survivors to share their narratives. Despite being hidden while in plain view since the disaster in 2005, the best way to end this book is in the voices of these Mississippi Hurricane Katrina Black women survivors so that they have agency to describe and explain where they are today.

Helen, Gulfport, Mississippi
We were overlooked right after the storm and still are nationally each year. Regardless of that, Mississippians did not give up, and we continue to get better each year.

Jean, Biloxi, Mississippi
Katrina was devastating, but it was a blessing too. See, I have seen women stepping up and trying to make sure their communities are sustained. They were not doing that before the storm. Women at [private agency name] have stepped up to. They are advocating for themselves, and they were definitely not in that space at all before Katrina.

Mary, Gulfport, Mississippi
For me and many people I know here on the Mississippi Gulf Coast, there is life after Katrina.

Sam, Pass Christian, Mississippi
We are ALIVE [emphasis added]!!! We're together, nobody in our family died. We are so fortunate. It made me reevaluate my life.

I want to spend time with my sons and my grandkids. I want to do things in my community. I have never had more clarity in my life.

Laura, Gulfport, Mississippi
I want [everyone] to know that we are very thankful for all that you have done for us, like bringing water, food, or coming to see about us, or whatever else you did. We are grateful for your help. Also, I want people to know that—that—there is recovery *after* disaster.

Catherine, Pass Christian, Mississippi
Experiencing Katrina was like a new birth. You know, when you have a child, they are with you for the rest of your life. The eruption of Katrina was like a new child. You start out fresh; it has to grow. It cannot stay stagnant—change will occur. I have changed and continue to change each day: the Katrina reality.

APPENDIX

RESEARCH DESIGN
Methods

THE PRIMARY TYPES OF DATA collection methods used in this study were the snowball technique, interviews (in person and via the telephone), secondary sources, participant observation, and emic perspective. Each will be discussed in this section. According to sociologist and disaster scholar Robert Merton (1970), the snowball method is useful to secure participants after natural disasters or other catastrophic events. The snowball method (Phillips, 2014; Goodman, 1961) generated the sample of women in Mississippi. After receiving the women's names from alliances on the Mississippi Gulf Coast, each woman was contacted in person and via telephone about participating in the study about Hurricane Katrina survivors and to schedule a time for a personal interview. All interviews were conducted by the author. The women volunteered to participate in this study and agreed to be audio-taped prior to each recorded session with no coercion.

Interview protocol

The most commonly used research method with survivors after natural disasters is interviews. All of the interviews in this study were conducted by the author and used a semi-structured (Strauss & Corbin, 2007) approach. The initial and follow-up interviews were digitally audio-recorded. All of the women gave their consent and agreed to be interviewed before any interview questions were asked. The interview questions related to the women's experiences before, during, and since Hurricane Katrina. First, each woman was asked for demographic information such as her name, age, and city of residence before and after the hurricane. The women were asked questions about their knowledge of the approaching hurricane and how they used that information. Then they were asked to describe their actions as the storm approached and what they did after Hurricane Katrina. Also, the women were asked to describe any changes in their lives since the disaster. During follow-up interviews, questions were based on comments the women had made in previous years on subjects such as damage or repairs to their homes, insurance claims, or their employment status. In addition, the women were asked about their thoughts on the economic climate and regional recovery, as well as a plethora of other questions both planned and impromptu, which were generated from the comments they made. Lastly, the women were asked to discuss any information that they thought or felt was important that had not been addressed. Each interview lasted between forty-five and 130 minutes, with the average session being about seventy-five minutes.

Triangulation

In addition to interviews, several unobtrusive (Webb, 1999) secondary and tertiary methods were used to augment these Mississippi women's accounts through triangulation (Flick, 2007; Guba, 1981; Denzin, 1970). These sources included books, newspaper articles, DVD documentaries, regional photography, and personal observation. Each method added authenticity and proved dependable as they reinforced the women's interview data. During my visits to Mississippi, I located documentaries and DVDs, most notably, *Gulf Coast Disaster— Hurricane Katrina—Mississippi Hancock County* (2005) that was produced by WLOX, the leading Mississippi Gulf

Coast TV station, which provided day-by-day reports of the disaster. Local newspaper articles from *The Sun Herald* (Gulfport, Mississippi) and *The Times Picayune* (Slidell, Louisiana) provided a plethora of regional and local information about Mississippi Hurricane Katrina survivors that did not make the national news and corroborated many of the comments made by women in the study. These sources provided meaningful facts about what was happening on the ground in Mississippi after the disaster. What's more, this form of triangulation is used to buttress the trustworthiness (Bates, 2014) of the women's interview data. There were several other graphic sources, such as *Katrina: Eight Hours That Changed the Mississippi Coast Forever* (2005) and many others that discussed the impact of Hurricane Katrina in Mississippi on survivors. According to Bogdan and Biklen (1992), pictures tell stories that words cannot convey. Regional Gulf Coast bookstores sold local photographers' postcards and magazines depicting how the Mississippi Gulf Coast looked before and after Hurricane Katrina. The images in the sources added veracity to the women's descriptions and provided greater insight into the disaster's impact on survivors and the region. In addition, I met with some of the women in this case study over lunch or dinner and have seen others at Hurricane Katrina anniversary events over the years. These relaxed conversations added breadth and depth to the interview data. Also, my time with the women allowed me to observe them and write a plethora of field notes, which provided a fuller picture of their lived experiences. Lastly, I drove across the Mississippi Gulf Coast from Hancock through Harrison to Jackson County during my visits to the area. While there, I drove through the women's neighborhoods in Pass Christian, Gulfport, and Biloxi to get a sense (Guilette, 1993) of how the Gulf Coast was rebounding. My trips to the Mississippi Gulf Coast continue to serve as an ongoing observational strategy that provides valuable information about the women's and the region's recovery.

Data Analysis

After the interviews were transcribed, grounded theory principles (Corbin and Strauss, 2008; Glaser and Strauss, 2000) were used to begin the analysis process. Each like-response (Moustakas, 1994) on the transcripts was color coded (Corbin and Strauss, 2008; Strauss & Corbin, 1998) for easy recognition. The codes from multiple like-responses led to the emergence of patterns. During this process, several conceptual categories emerged as I began to see how the women's experiences paralleled and complemented one another. Several themes emerged after teasing out patterns. A few of the themes were analogous to those found in women's disaster literature, such as the emergence of female leaders (Enarson and Morrow, 1998), experiences with FEMA in New Orleans (Mason, 2012), the loss of personal property and homes (Enarson and Morrow, 1998), and feeling overwhelmed (Fothergill, 2004). In addition, several new themes specific to these Black women Hurricane Katrina survivors emerged, such as the women's employment dilemma after the storm and their "I will rise above this" attitude (Angelou, 1978), which is analogous to a Womanist (Walker, 1984) tenet, one of the frameworks that grounds this study. A second theme was the women's emphasis on the importance of helping each other and their communities get through the aftermath of the storm and recovery. Third, the women expressed feelings of gratitude for the help that their communities received from the volunteers over the years to rebuild the Mississippi Gulf Coast. During the second round of interviews, I probed the women for clarifications from the first interviews and asked new questions. This was done to test the strength of the findings, a process known as "constant comparative analysis" (Corbin and Strauss, 2007; Glaser & Strauss, 2000). This strategy allowed me to use my original findings from the 2005 interviews as a baseline to analyze new data as the women shared their ongoing experiences each year after Hurricane Katrina. As the data was collapsed (Hill et al., 2005) in an ongoing simultaneous (Charmez, 1995), interwoven, cyclical, and dynamic analytical process (Corbin and Strauss, 2007; Glaser and Strauss,

2000; Lofland and Lofland, 1984), the analysis was substantiated and yielded new themes. In 2012, after constantly comparing the data, "theoretical saturation" (Corbin and Strauss, 2007; Glaser & Strauss, 2000) was reached because the women were repeating major themes from previous years and interviews as their concerns started to shift since most of their lives were beginning to resemble the middle-class lifestyles to which they were accustomed before Hurricane Katrina. Women disaster scholars Jenkins and Phillips (2008) used a similar strategy where "... findings were checked by comparing them to issues raised by the advocates and survivors..." (p. 56). Finally, to eliminate misinterpretation of the women's words, each woman reviewed her transcripts to clarify that what she said was accurately stated.

Summary

The primary method used in this study was in-depth interviews. Secondary and tertiary methods served as fact-checking sources to fortify the findings. Observation (Phillips, 2014; Goodman, 1961) was used because it accurately reveals human behavior in its most natural state, and it enables people to drop their guard and become genuine (Kottak, 2006; Corden and Sainsbury, 2005). This process allows researchers to capture data in real time, which is very different from that gathered in positivistic designs (Corbin and Strauss, 2014). In fact, observation yields thick and rich data with attention to tacit information (Grady, 1998). Triangulation (Bryman, 2014; Flick, 1992) enhances the authenticity (Erlandson et al., 1993) of research data and findings. This technique allows the comparisons of interview data with personal observations, while drawing parallels from DVD documentaries to ultimately ensure precise analysis. Lastly, the women's interview comments were compared to reports from regional newspaper articles to ensure significance and veracity. Since comprehensive studies are nonexistent, the next section will discuss this study's limitations.

Limitations

Because quantitative researchers have traditionally held biased views on qualitative strategies, this section clarifies its authenticity. One's personal attributes, such as birth or ethnicity, are referred to in the literature as emic perspective (Kottak, 2006). I was born in Greenwood, Mississippi, in the central part of the state known as the Delta, and am a Black American woman. Like many women scholars of color (Hurston, 2018; Collins, 1998; Clark-Hine, 1995; Thornton-Dill, 1994; Crenshaw, 1991; Walker, 1983; Petry, 1946), insider, or emic, perspective (Kottak, 2006) enabled me to report the findings from the data as an enlightened investigator. To reduce personal bias, as an ethical researcher, I remained committed to report the findings from the data analysis to bring the women's voices to the forefront, not my own. Corden and Sainsbury (2005) report that using longer than usual quotations in manuscripts assist in this process. My primary goal was to write up the findings in the women's words to give them a voice and agency to ensure that their experiences were clear to readers. One example of ethical emic perspective is as follows. In 2005, prior to interviewing the Mississippi women, I thought that I would hear stories similar to those I heard and saw reported in the media immediately after Hurricane Katrina in New Orleans. But, after listening to the women during the interviews and reading the transcripts, I found that my initial thoughts were very different from the data. As an ethical researcher, I had to follow the data, not my personal opinion, so the data was coded and analyzed accordingly. As a scholar with insider perspective, similar to the orientation of the women in this study—regionally and ethnically—my standpoint allowed me to bring a system of shared beliefs, values, practices, folk knowledge, language norms, rituals, and affinity to the group under investigation (Kottak, 2006). Although it was once viewed skeptically, over the past fifty years, insider perspective has become an accepted, meaningful, and reliable approach. In fact, according to Banks (1998), being an indigenous researcher enables one to offer a unique perspective that has been overlooked historically and is often missing in contemporary studies that include people of color. Moreover, Banks (1998) says, the indigenous insider is viewed as "a legitimate member of the community who has the perspective and the knowledge that will promote the well-being of the community, enhance its power, and enable it to maintain cultural integrity and survive" (p. 7-8). Further, insider perspective (Kottak, 2006; Denzin and Lincoln, 2005) or doctrine (Merton, 1976) is advantageous because subjects tend to be authentic when relating to researchers who share their background and experience. This kinship (Collins, 1998) or understanding of groups enhances credible findings (Kottak, 2006). Moreover, qualitative researchers view insider perspective positively because it strengthens findings (Kottak, 2006; Denzin and Lincoln, 2005). Barber and Haney's (2015) study confirmed that the scarcity of researchers with insider perspective in disaster studies is a major problem that needs to be addressed to ensure that survivors authentic voices are heard correctly. Finally, while it is good to have researchers conduct studies and write books, scholars, experts, and amateurs should know that, as Anna Julia Cooper (1892) communicated in her book, *A Voice from the South by A Black Woman of the South*, emic researchers know the experiences of those in their community and can tell their stories better than outsiders.

Regarding generalizability, no study is one hundred percent precise. This qualitative longitudinal case study represents the voices of these Mississippi Hurricane Katrina Black women survivors, not the plight of all women from the Mississippi Gulf Coast. The final limitation in this study concerns the psychological impact Hurricane Katrina had on survivors. This book contains only a brief discussion of the topic for several reasons. First, there are a number of studies (Patel, 2012; Rhodes, Chan, Paxson, Rouse, Waters, and Fussell, 2010; Jenick, 2010; Davis, Elder, Grills-Tagueche, and Ollendick, 2010) on this topic. Secondly, neither am I licensed to administer psychological tests nor did I have a test administered to these women.

During the interviews, I received limited data about the topic from the women. Rather than concentrate on a frequently studied aspect of disasters, namely psychological trauma, instead I chose, one, to add new knowledge to the disaster canon about the last stage of disasters—resilience and recovery—and two, to investigate a never-studied group of Black women survivors by following the data I collected. This is not to say that that is not important because it is, but it was simply not the focus of this book.

ACKNOWLEDGEMENTS

THERE ARE SEVERAL PEOPLE who provided encouragement and support to help me keep working until this project was complete. Without your support and stability, this project would have been much more difficult to complete. To the reference librarians who helped me secure articles, books, and documentaries. You played a vital part in the process and completion of this project. Thank you, David Blustein and Marie Land, for helping me get this project started. Thanks, Northeastern University Women's Studies Department for valuing my work and providing a fellowship opportunity and resources for me develop the project. Thank you former colleagues Julie Norem, Kelly Rutherford Breland, and Layli Maparyan, for believing in my work when many did not. Filomina Steady and Kelly Carter Jackson, you were good colleagues, and I appreciate you both more than you will ever know. To my friends and family who cheered me on: Lynn Benson, Mary Szoto, Joanne Whitaker, Maurine Daw, Sharon Walcott, Sasha Coleman-Johnson, and Conner, I appreciate each of you so much!! To my sisters Lena, Gerri, Ros, Chelle, Audrey, and Tiwanna, and my brother Steve, I hope my work makes you proud. My first editor, Brian you helped me get the book ready for submission and your work on the volume helped open the door for acceptance. To Koehler Books: John, thanks for taking a chance on me and returning my telephone call. Joe, it has been great to work with you as the book moved through the final stages before going to print. Working with Koehler has been a wonderful experience, and I look forward to working with you again. Danielle, my website designer, you are very talented and did a great job on the website. To my copyeditor, popular author, Jessica Meigs, Koehler chose one of the best to take this book to the next level. It has been a dream come true to work with you, Jessica—thank you so much! To my award-winning cover designer, Skyler your work speaks for itself! To my prayer partners, Cheryl Jordan and Iver Gandy, God heard and answered our prayers. Thank you so much for praying this book through to publication. Bonnie Thornton Dill, without your guidance over the years, I know it would have been very difficult for me to finish this book. You suggested ways to think about grounding the study. You accepted all of my calls and responded to my emails quickly. Thank you, Bonnie, over and over again. Thank you, Mississippi Black women Katrina survivors, for allowing me to write your stories. Lastly and most importantly, to God my Father: Thank you for leading me to the project and helping me complete it. May it be a Blessings to many. Amen.

REFERENCES

Ager, Alastair and Maryanne Loughry. 2004. Psychology and Humanitarian Assistance. *Journal of Humanitarian Assistance.* http://sites.tufts.edu/jha/archives/80

Alan, Jamie, Michael Moore, Ryan Denney, Tania Bayne, Amy Stagg, Stacy Owens, Samantha Daniels, Stefanie Boswell, Jane Schenck, Jason Adams, and Charissa Jones. 2008. God Images Following Hurricane Katrina in South Mississippi: An Exploratory Study. *Journal of Psychology and Theology* Winter, 2008.

Anastario, Michael, Nadine Shehab and Lynn Lawry. 2009. Increased Gender-Based Violence Among Women Internally Displaced in Mississippi two years Post-Hurricane Katrina. *Disaster Medicine and Public Health Preparedness* 3, 18-26.

Anderson, Ellis. 2010. *Under Surge Under Siege: The Odyssey of Bay St. Louis and Katrina.* Jackson: University of Mississippi Press.

Angel, Robert J., Holly Bell, Julie Beausoleil, and Laura Lein. 2012. *The State, Civil Society, and Displaced Survivors of Hurricane Katrina.* Cambridge University Press.

Angelou, Maya. 1978. *And Still I Rise.* NY: Random House.

Antoine, Rebeca. 2008. *Voice Rising Stories from the Katrina Narrative Project*. New Orleans: UNO Press.

Arnold, Christopher. 1993. *Reconstruction After Earthquakes: Issues, Urban Design, and Case Studies*. Report to National Science Foundation, Building Systems Development, Inc. San Mateo, California.

Asante, Molefi Kete. 2018. The History of Africa: The Quest for Eternal Harmony 3rd edition. NY: Routledge.

Bakhtin, Mikhail, M. 1981. *The Dialogic Imagination: In Four Essays*. University of Texas Press.

Banks, J. A. 1998. The Lives and Values of Researchers: Implications for Educating Citizens in a Multicultural Society. *Education Research*, 27, 4–17.

Bamberg, Michael. 2012. Narrative Analysis, In H. Cooper (Ed). *APA Handbook of Research Methods in Psychology*. Washington: American Psychological Association.

Barber, Kristen and Timothy J Haney. 2015. The experiential gap in disaster research: Feminist epistemology and the contribution of local affected researchers. Sociological Spectrum 57-74.

Barbour, Haley. 2015. *America's Great Storm: Leading Through Hurricane Katrina*. Jackson: University of Mississippi Press.

Barbour, Haley. 2005. Governor's Commission on Recovery, Rebuilding, and Renewal, After Katrina: Building Back Better Than Ever. *Governor's Commission Report*. 60-61.

Barnshaw, John and Joseph Trainor. 2010. Race, Class, and Capital Amidst the Hurricane Katrina Diaspora. In David Brunsma, David Overfelt, and J. Stephen Picou (Eds), *The Sociology of Katrina: Perspectives on a Modern Catastrophe*, Second Edition. Lanham, MD: Rowman and Littlefield.

Barnshaw, John and Joseph Trainor. 2007. Race, Class, and Capital Amidst the Hurricane Katrina Diaspora. In David Brunsma, David Overfelt, and J. Stephen Picou (Eds), *The Sociology of Katrina: Perspectives on a Modern Catastrophe*. Lanham, MD: Rowman and Littlefield. 95-105.

Barry, John M. 1998. *Rising Tide: The Great Mississippi Flood of 1927 and How It Changed America*. La Jolla: Simon & Schuster.

Barusch, Amanda. 2012. Refining The Narrative Turn: When Does Story-Telling Become Research? *Gerontological Society of American.*

Barton, Allen. 1969. *Communities in Disaster: A Sociological Analysis of Collective Stress Situation.* NY: Doubleday.

Bates, Tiffany. 2014. *The Survival Experiences of Black Women in New Orleans During and after Hurricane Katrina.* Houston: Sam Houston State University.

Beady, Jr., C.H. and R.C. Bolin. 1986. The Role of the Black Media in Disaster Reporting to the Black Community. Working Paper No. 56 Institute for Behavioral Science, University of Colorado, Boulder as cited in Fothergill, Maestas, and Darlington (Eds), *Race, Ethnicity and Disasters in the United States: A Review of the Literature, Disasters,* 1999, 23 (2):156-173.

Begum, Recede. 1993. Women in Environmental Disasters: The 1991 Cyclone in Bangladesh. *Focus on Gender* 1 (1): 34-39. bell hooks. 2000. *Feminist Theory: From the Margins to the Center*. Boston: South End Press.

Bell, Randall and Donald T. Phillips. 2006. *Disasters: Wasted Lives, Valuable Lessons*. Dallas: Tapestry Press.

Berry, Chester. 2005. *Loss of the Sultana and Reminiscences of Survivors: Voices of the Civil War. Knoxville*: University of Tennessee Press.

Bogdan, Robert. C. & Sari Knopp Biklen. 1992. *Qualitative Research for Education: An Introduction to Theory and Methods*. Boston: Allyn and Bacon.

Bolin, Bob. 2006. Race, Class, Ethnicity, and Disaster Vulnerability. In *Handbook of Disaster Research*, Havidan Rodriguez, Enrico Quarantelli and Russel Dynes (Eds). NY: Springer Press, 113-129.

Bolin, Robert. C. and Lois Stanford. 1996. Cultural Diversity, Unmet Needs, and Disaster Recovery: The Northridge Earthquake. Pan Pacific Hazards 96 Meeting as cited in Enarson and Hearn (Eds) *The Gendered Terrain of Disaster: Through Women's Eyes*. Vancouver, BC, July 28 to August 2.

Bourdieu, Pierre. 2009. The Forms of Capital in Jeff Manza and Micheal Sauder (Eds) *Inequality and Society Social Science Perspectives on Social Stratification*, 443-456. NY: Norton.

Bourdieu, Pierre. 1994. *Distinction: A Social Critique of the Judgment of Taste. In David* Grusky (Ed) Social Stratification Class, Race, and Gender in Social Perspectives, 404-430. Boulder: Westview.

Bowles, Tuere A., Monica Terrell Leach, Pamela P. Martin, Tuere A. Bowles and Jocelyn DeVance Taliaferro. 2008. Our Souls Look Back in Wonder: The Spirituality of African American Families Surviving Katrina. In Dorothy M. Singleton *The aftermath of Katrina: Educating Traumatized Children Pre-K to College.* Maryland: University Press of America.

Bowser, Benjamin. 2007. *The Black Middle Class: Social Mobility and Vulnerability.* Boulder: Rienner Press.

Brinkley, Douglas. 2006. *The Great Deluge: Hurricane Katrina, New Orleans, and the Mississippi Gulf Coast.* NY: Harper Collins.

Brown, Roger. 1976. *A First Language: The Early Stages.* Boston: Harvard Press.

Brunsma, David, David Overfelt, and Steven Picou. 2010. *The Sociology of Katrina: Perspectives on a Modern Catastrophe* Second edition. Lanham, MD: Rowman & Littlefield.

Brunsma, David, David Overfelt, and Steven Picou. 2007. *The Sociology of Katrina: Perspectives on a Modern Catastrophe.* Lanham, MD: Rowman & Littlefield.

Bryman, A. n.d. Triangulation. http://www.referenceworld.com/ sage/socialscience/triangulation.pdf Accessed October 13, 2014.

Bryne-Armstrong, Hilary. 2001. Whose Show Is it? The Contradiction of Collaboration in Hilary Bryne-Armstrong, Joy Higgs and Debbie Horsfall (Eds), Critical Moments in Qualitative Research. Butterworth Heinemann, Oxford, 106-112.

Bullard, Robert and Beverly Wright. 2009. *Race, Place, and Environmental Justice After Hurricane Katrina: Struggles to Reclaim, Rebuild, and Revitalize New Orleans and the Gulf Coast.* Boulder: Westview Press.

Bureau of Labor Statistics. 2006. Quarterly Census of Employment and Wages. Monthly Labor Review. Accessed January, 15, 2007.

Burt, Ronald. 1997. The Contingent Value of Social Capital. *Administrative Sciences Quarterly.* 42, 2 339-2365.

Butler, Octavia. 1993. The Parable of the Sower. Grand Central Publishing.

Calloway, Candace M. 2009. *News Media, Black Women, and Hurricane Katrina: Comparing Localized Content to Local Perceptions.* Washington, DC: Howard University ProQuest UMI Dissertation Publishing.

Cannon, Katie. 1996. *Katie's Canon Womanism and the Soul of the Black Community.* NY: New York Continuum.

Cayton, Horace and St. Clair Drake. 1945. *Black Metropolis.* Harcourt Brace & Company.

Central Mississippi Planning and Development District. 2009. *Demographic Data.* Accessed December 30, 2009, http://www.cmpdd.org/demographic_data.php

Charmaz, K. 2009. Shifting the Grounds: Constructivist Grounded Theory Methods. In J. M. Morse, P. N. Stern, J. Corbin, B. Bowers, K. Charmaz, & A. E. Clarke (Eds.), *Developing Grounded Theory: The Second Generation* 127–154). Walnut Creek: Left Coast Press.

Charmaz, Kathy. 1995. The Body, Identity and Self. *The Sociological Quarterly*, 36, 657-680.

Cladinin, D. Jean and Michael F. Connolly. 2000. *Narrative Inquiry: Experiences in Qualitative Research*. San Francisco: Jossey-Bass.

Clason, Christine. 1983. The Family as a Life-Saver in Disasters. *Journal of Mass Emergencies and Disasters*. 1:1, 43-62.

Collins, Patricia Hill. 2000. *Black Feminist Thought: Knowledge, Consciousness, and the Politics of Empowerment*. New York: Routledge.

Collins, Patricia Hill. 1998. *Fighting Words: Black Women and The Search for Justice*. Minneapolis: University of Minnesota Press.

Cooper, Anna Julia. 1892. *A Voice From the South*. Xenia, Ohio: The Aldine Printing House.

Corden, Anne and Roy Sainsbury. 2005. Verbatim Quotations in Applied Social Research: Theory, Practice and Impact. *Social Policy Research Unit*. England: University of York. Assessed January 5, 2006 https://pure.york.ac.uk/portal/en/projects/verbatim-quotations-in-applied-social-research-theory-practice-and-impact(c24a44ff-c114-4d74-a1f6-b748acfa66cc).html

Conyers, James L. 2016. *Qualitative Methods in Africana Studies: An Interdisciplinary Approach to Examining Africana Phenomenon*. Lanham: University Press of America.

Corbin, Juliet & Anselm Strauss. 2014. *Basics of Qualitative Research: Techniques and Procedures for Developing Grounded Theory*, Fourth Edition. Thousand Oaks: Sage.

Corbin, Juliet & Anselm Strauss. 2008. *Basics of Qualitative Research: Techniques and Procedures for Developing Grounded Theory*, Third Edition. Thousand Oaks: Sage.

Crawford, Vicki. 1993. *Women and Civil Rights Movement: Trailblazers and Torchbearers, 1941-1965*. Bloomington: Indiana Press.

Cram, Bridgette. 2014. *Women in the Face of Disaster: Incorporating Gender Perspectives into disaster Policy*. Quick Response Grant Report series, 247.

Crenshaw, Kimberle Williams. 1991. Demarginalizing the Intersection of Race and Sex: Black Feminist Critique of Discrimination Doctrine, Feminist Theory and Anti-Racist Politics. In Katherine Bartlett and Rosanne Kennedy (Eds) *Feminist Legal Theory*. Boulder: Westview Press.

Creswell, John. 2013. *Research Design: Qualitative, Quantitative, and Mixed Methods Approaches*, Fourth Edition. Thousand Oaks: Sage.

Cutter, Susan, Christopher Emrich, Jerry Mitchell, Walter Piegorsch, Mark Smith and Lynn Weber. 2014. *Hurricane Katrina and the Forgotten Mississippi Gulf Coast*. New York: Routledge.

Cutter, Susan, Christopher Emrich, Jerry Mitchell, Bryan Boruff, Melanie Gall, Mathew Schmidtlein, Christopher Burton and Ginne Melton. 2006. The Long Road Home:

Race, Class, and Recovery from Hurricane Katrina. *Environment* 48:2 8-20.

Cutter, Susan. 2006. The Geography of Social Vulnerability: Race, Class and Catastrophe. *Understanding Katrina: Perspectives from the Social Sciences, Accessed December 15, 2006* http:// understandingkatrina.ssrc.org/Cutter

Cutter, Susan. 2005. The Geography of Social Vulnerability: Race, Class and Catastrophe, in Understanding Katrina: Perspectives from the Social Sciences. *Social Science Research Council.* Accessed December 29, 2005 https://items.ssrc.org/ understanding-katrina/the-geography-of-social-vulnerability- race-class-and-catastrophe/

Cutter, Susan. 1995. The Forgotten Casualties: Women, Children and Environmental Change, *Global Environmental Change: Human and Policy Dimensions* 5:3 181-194.

Daniel, Pete. 1977. *Deep'n As It Come: The 1927 Mississippi Flood.* New York: Oxford Press.

David, Emmanuel. 2017. *Women of the Storm: Civic Activism After Hurricane Katrina.* Chicago: University of Illinois Press.

David, Emmanuel and Elaine Enarson. 2012. *The Women of Katrina: How Gender, Race, and Class Matter in An American Disaster.* Nashville: Vanderbilt Press.

David, Emmanuel. 2010. Studying Up on Women and Disaster: An Elite Sustained Women's Group Following Hurricane Katrina. *International Journal of Mass Emergencies and Disasters,* 28:2, 246–269.

David, Emmanuel. 2009. *Women of the Storm: An Ethnography of Gender, Culture, and Social Movements Following Hurricane Katrina.* Denver: University of Colorado ProQuest UMI Dissertation Publishing Accessed January 20, 2009.

Davidson, Charles. 2006. The Gulf Coast's Tourism Comeback: Playing for Even Higher Stakes. *Econ South*, 8, 3.

Davis III, Thomas Elder, Amie Grills-Taquechel, and Thomas Ollendick. 2010. The Psychological Impact from Hurricane Katrina: Effects of Displacement on College Students. *Behavior Therapy*, 41, 340-349.

Davis, Ophera. 2008. Stories from Women Survivors of Hurricane Katrina. *Proceedings from the Ninth Annual Diversity Challenge* - Boston College.

Davis, Ophera and Land, Marie. 2007. One-Year-Later: Southern Women Voices on Hurricane Katrina. *Journal of Race, Gender, and Class, 14:1-2, 68-86.*

Davis, Ophera and Land, Marie. 2006. Southern Women Vices from the Gulf Coast States on Hurricane Katrina. Harvard University - *Journal of African-American Public Policy* XII, 9-16.

DemographicsNow. 2005. Statistics on Mississippi Women *DemographicsNow* (subscription needed). http://library. demographicsnow.com

Denzin, Norman. and Yvonna Lincoln. 2005. *The Sage Handbook of Qualitative Research.* Thousand Oaks: Sage.

Denzin, Norman. 1970. *The Research Act: A Theoretical Introduction to Sociological Methods.* Chicago: Aldine Publishing Company.

Deweever, Avis Jones. 2011. The Forgotten Ones: Black Women in the Wake of Katrina. In Cedric Johnson (Ed) *The Neoliberal Deluge: Hurricane Katrina, Late Capitalism, and the Remaking of New Orleans.* University of Minnesota Press. 300-326.

Deweever, Avis Jones. 2008. Women in the Wake of the Storm: Examining the Post-Katrina Realities of the Women of New Orleans and the Gulf Coast. *Institute for Women's Policy Research.* Washington DC. Accessed January 21, 2009 http://www.iwpr. org/initiatives/katrina-the-gulf-coast#sthash.clryIr1N.dpuf

Dikkers, R.D. 1971. *Hurricane Camille—August 1969.* Ann Arbor: University of Michigan.

Dill, Bonnie Thornton and R. E. Zambrana. 2009. *Emerging Intersections: Race, Class, and Gender in Theory, Policy, and Practice.* Rutgers: Rutgers University Press.

Dill, Bonnie Thornton. 1998. A Better Life for Me and My Children. *Journal of Comparative Family Studies,* 419-428.

Dill, Bonnie Thornton. 1993. *Across the Boundaries of Race and Class: An Exploration of Work and Family Among Black Female Domestic Workers.* NY: Garland Publishing.

Dill, Bonnie Thornton. 1992. *Race gender and poverty in the Rural South.: African American Single Mothers.* In Cynthia Duncan (Ed) Rural Poverty in America. Westport: Auburn House.

Dill, Bonnie Thornton. 1988. Our Mother's Grief: Racial Ethnic Women and the Maintenance of Families. *Journal of Family History Center for Research on Women, Memphis State University,* 13: 1, 415-431.

Drabek, Thomas. and K. Boggs. 1968. Families in Disaster: Reactions and Relatives. *Journal of Marriage and the Family.* 8: 443-51.

Drake, St. Clair & Cayton, Horace R. 1945. *Black Metropolis: A Study of Negro Life in a Northern City.* Chicago: University of Chicago.

Dubois, W.E.B. 1903. *Souls of Black Folks.* Chicago: AC McClurg.

Dyson, Michael Eric. 2006. *Come Hell or High Water: Hurricane Katrina and the Color of a Disaster.* Cambridge: Basic Books.

Elliott, James, R and Jeremy Pais. 2006. Race, Class and Hurricane Katrina: Social Differences in Human Responses to Disaster. *Social Science Research,* 35, 295-321.

Elliott, James W. 1962. *Transport to Disaster: The Forgotten Story of Sunken Sultana in Mississippi.* New York: Holt, Rinehart, and Winston.

Enarson, Elaine, Alice Fothergill and Lori Peek. 2007. Gender and Disaster: Foundations and Directions. In Havidán A. Rodríguez, Enrico Quarantelli, and Russell Dynes (Eds) *Handbook of Disaster Research.* New York: Springer.

Enarson, Elaine. 2012. *Women Confronting Natural Disasters: Social Issues and Initiatives.* Thousand Oaks: Sage.

Enarson, Elaine, 2010. *Personal Communication*, National Women's Studies Association Conference.

Enarson, Elaine and Betty Hearn Morrow. 1998. *The Gendered Terrain Disaster: Through Women's Eyes.* Westport: Greenwood Publishing.

Erlandson, David, Edward Harris, Barbara Skipper, and Steven Allen. 1993. *Doing Naturalistic Inquiry: A Guide To Methods.* Thousand Oaks: Sage.

Erickson, Kai and Lori Peek. 2009. Hurricane Katrina Research Bibliography. *Social Science Research Bibliography.* http:// katrinaresearchhub.ssrc.org/Katrinabibliography, Accessed November 15, 2009.

Erickson, Kai. 1976. *Everything In Its Path: Destruction of Community in the Buffalo Creek Flood.* New York: Simon and Schuster.

Federal Emergency Management Agency (FEMA). 2005. Hurricane Katrina Information. http://www.fema.gov/hazard/ hurricane/2005katrina/index.shtm Accessed December 15, 2005.

Flick, Uwe. 2007. Triangulation. *Journal for the Theory of Social Behavior,* 22: 2. Accessed July 1, 2007.

Flick, Uwe. 1992. Triangulation Revisited: Strategy of Validation or Alternative? *Journal for the Theory of Social Behavior,* 22:2, 175-197.

Fitzhugh, Dorothy, John Wilson, and Drew Tarter. 2006. *Katrina: Before and After* First Edition. Gulfport: Sun Herald.

Fordham, Maureen. 1999. The Intersection of Gender and Social Class in Disaster: Balancing Resilience and Vulnerability. *International Journal of Mass Emergencies and Disasters,* 17: 1 15-36.

Fordham, Maureen. 1998. Making Women Visible in Disasters: Problematising the Private Domain. *Disasters.* 22: 2.

Fothergill, Alice. 2004. *Heads Above Water: Gender, Class, and Family in the Grand Forks Flood.* New York: SUNY.

Fothergill, Anne, Enrique Maestas and Joanne Darlington. 1999. Race, Ethnicity and Disasters in the United States: A Review of the Literature. *Disasters* 23: 2, 156-173.

Fothergill, Alice. 1998. The Neglect of Gender in Disaster Work: An Overview of the Literature. In Elaine Enarson and Betty Hearn Morrow (Eds) *The Gendered Terrain of Disaster: Through Women's Eyes.* Westport: Praeger.

Fothergill, Alice. 1996. Gender, Risk and Disaster. *International Journal of Mass Emergencies and Disasters* 14: 1, 33-56.

Fritz, Charles. 1961. Disasters. *In* Robert Merton and Robert Nisbet (Eds) *Contemporary Social Problems.* New York: Harcourt, Brace and World.

Fritz, Charles and Eli Marks. 1954. The NORC Studies of Human Behavior in Disasters. *Journal of Social Issues,* 10: 26-41.

Gafford, Farrah, D. 2010. *Life in the Park: Community Solidarity, Culture, and the Case of a Black Middle-Class Neighborhood.* New Orleans: Tulane University ProQuest UMI Dissertation Publishing.

Gafford, Farrah, D. 2010 Rebuilding the Park: The Impact of Hurricane Katrina on a Middle-Class Black Neighborhood. *Journal of Black Studies*, 41: 2, 385-404.

Gault, Barbara, Heidi Hartmann, Avis Jones-DeWeever, Misha Werschkul, and Erica Williams. 2005. The Women of New Orleans and the Gulf Coast: Multiple Disadvantages and KeyAssets for Recovery Part I. Poverty, Race, Gender and Class. *Institute for Women's Policy Research*. Publication No. D464. Washington DC.

Gergen, Mary and Kenneth Gergen. 1984. The Social Construction of Narrative Accounts. In Gergen, Mary and Kenneth Gergen (Eds) *Historical Social Psychology*. Englewood: Lawrence Erlbaum Publishers.

Giddings Paula. 1985. *When and Where I Enter: The Impact of Black Women on Race and Sex in America*. NY: Bantam.

Giddings, Paula. 2007. *When and Where I Enter: The Impact of Black Women on Race and Sex in America*. Second Edition. New York: William Morrow.

Gilkes, Cheryl Townsend. 1985. Together and in Harness: Women's Traditions in the Sanctified Church. *Signs* 10: 4, 678-699.

Gilkes, Cheryl Townsend. 2001. *If It Wasn't For the Women: Black Women's Experience and Womanist Culture in Church and Community*. Maryknoll: Orbis.

Gilligan, Carol. 1982. *In a Different Voice: Psychological Theory and Women's Development*. Cambridge: Harvard Press.

Gladwin, Hugh and Walter Peacock. 1997. Warning and Evacuation: A Night for Hard Houses. In Walter Peacock, Hugh Gladwin and Betty Hearn Morrow (Eds), *Hurricane Andrew: Ethnicity, Gender, and the Sociology of Disasters*, 52-74. NY: Routledge.

Glaser, Barney and Anselm Strauss. 2000. *The Discovery of Grounded Theory: Strategies for Qualitative Research*. NY: Routledge.

Grady, Michael P. 1998. *Qualitative and Action Research: A Practitioner Handbook*. Bloomington: Phi Delta Kappa.

Gray-White, Deborah. 1985. *A'rn't I a Woman: Female Slaves in the Plantation South*. New York: Norton.

Golding, Melody and Sally Pister. 2007. *Katrina: Mississippi Women Remember*. Jackson: University of Mississippi Press.

Goodman, Leo A. 1961. Snowball Sampling. *The Annals of Math Statistics*. 32:1 148-170.

Goodman, Leo A. 2011. Comment: On Respondent-Driven Sampling and Snowball Sampling in Hard-To-Reach Populations and Snowball Sampling Not In Hard-To-Reach-Populations. *Sociological Methodology*, 41, 347-353.

Green, Bonnie L. 1993. Mental Health and Disaster: Research Review. National Institute of Mental Health. *Violence and Traumatic Stress Research Branch*.

Grbich Carol. 1999. Qualitative Research in Health: An Introduction. As cited in Sally C. Hunter, Analysing and Representing Narrative Data: The Long and Winding Road, *Current Narratives* 2, 44-54.

Guba, Egon. G. 1981. Criteria for Assessing the Trustworthiness of Naturalistic Inquiries *Educational Communication and Technology Journal*, 29:2 75- 91.

Guest, Greg, Arwen Bunce and Laura Johnson. 2006. How Many Interviews are Enough? An Experiment with Data Saturation and Variability. *Field Methods*, 18: 59-82.

Guilette, E.A. 1993. The Role of the Aged in Community Recovery Following Hurricane Andrew.QR56. Quick Response Reports. Boulder: Natural Hazards Research and Application Information Center. In Walter Peacock, Hugh Gladwin and Betty Hearn Morrow (Eds), *Hurricane Andrew: Ethnicity, Gender, and the Sociology of Disasters*. NY: Routledge.

Guisepi, Robert A. 2003. Ancient Sumeria. Accessed March, 15, 2004, http://history-world.org/sumeria.htm

Hagan, F., J. Johnston, W. Monkhouse, and Kathryn Piquette. 2011. Narratives of Egypt and the Ancient Near East: Literary and Linguistic Approaches. *Orientalia Lovaniensia Analecta*. Walpole: Peeters.

Hall Joanne & Jill Powell. 2011. Understanding the Person through Narrative. *Nursing Research and Practice*, 1-10.

Haney, Timothy, James Elliot, and Elizabeth Fussell. 2010. Families and Hurricane Response: Risk, Roles, Resources, Race, and Religion: A Framework for Understanding Family Evacuation Strategies, Stress, and Return Mitigation. In David Brunsma, Dave Overfeldt and J. Steven Picou (Eds), The Sociology of Katrina: Perspectives on a Modern Catastrophe, 2nd Edition 77-102. Lanham, MD: Rowman and Littlefield.

Harley, Sharon and Sharon Taylor-Penn. 1997. *The Afro-American Woman: Struggle and Images.* Baltimore: Black Classic Press.

Harrison County Development Commission. 2007. Major Employers. *Harrison County Development Commission,* 73. Accessed January 20, 2008 http://mscoast.org/major-employers/major-employers/

Haubert, Jeanne and Elizabeth Russell. 2015. *Rethinking Disaster Recovery: A Hurricane Katrina Retrospective.* NY: Rowman and Littlefield.

Hearn, Phil. 2004. *Hurricane Camille: Monster Storm of the Gulf Coast.* Jackson: University of Mississippi Press.

Hess, Abigail. 2019. Closing the Gender Gap: This map shows which states have the biggest Gender Pay Gaps. *CNBC website,* Accessed June, 10, 2019. https://www.cnbc.com/2019/05/02/zippia-this-map-shows-which-states-have-the-biggest-gender-pay-gaps.html

Hewitt, Kenneth. 1995. Excluded Perspectives in the Social Construction of Disasters. *International Journal of Mass Emergencies and Disasters,* 13 3, 317-340.

Hill, Clara E, Barbara J. Thompson, Elizabeth Williams, Shirley A. Hess, Nicholas Ladany. 2005. Consensual Qualitative Research: An Update. *Journal of Counseling Psychology* 52: 2.

Hill, Marianne. 2008. *The Status of African Americans in Mississippi.* Center for Policy, Research, and Planning: Mississippi Institutions of Higher Learning.

Hines, Darlene Clark, Wilma King, and Linda Reed. 1995. *We Specialize in the Wholly Impossible: A Reader in Black Women's History*. NY: Carlson Publishing.

Hines-Datiri, Dorothy. 2017. Cloaked in Invisibility: Dropout-Recovery Narratives of Girls of Color after Re-enrollment. *Women, Gender, and Families of Color*, 5:1 27-49.

hooks, bell. 1993. *Sisters of the Yam: Black Women and Self-Recovery*. Boston, MA: South End.

hooks, bell. 1984. Feminist Theory: From Margin to Center. South End Press.

Hudson-Weems, Clenora. 2004. *Africana Womanism: Reclaiming Ourselves*, Fourth edition. Bedford Press, Lambertville, MI.

Hunter, Sally V. 2010. *Childhood Sexual Experiences: Narratives of Resilience*. Oxford: Radcliffe Publishing.

Hunter, Sally V. 2010. Analysing and Representing Narrative Data: The Long and Winding Road, *Current Narratives*, 2, 44-54.

Hunter, Tera. 1997. *To Joy My Freedom: Southern Black Women's Lives and Labors after the Civil War*. Cambridge: Harvard Press.

Hurricane Camille. 1969. National Hurricane Center. Accessed July 10, 2006 https://www.nhc.noaa.gov/news/20140401_pa_reanalysisCamille.pdf

Hurricane Katrina. 2005. National Hurricane Center. Accessed December 15, 2005 https://www.nhc.noaa.gov/archive/2005/pub/al122005.public.024.shtml?

Hurricane Katrina Memorial Mall. 2015. Biloxi Mississippi.

Hurston, Zora Neale. 2018. *Barracoon.* NY: Amistad Press.

Jencik, Alicia N. 2010. *Deconstructing Gender in New Orleans: The Impact of Patriarchy and Social Vulnerability Before and After a Natural Disaster.* University of New Orleans ProQuest UMI Dissertation Publishing.

Jenkins, Pam and Brenda Phillips, 2008. Battered Women, Catastrophe, and the Context of Safety after Hurricane Katrina. *National Women's Studies Association Journal* 20: 3, 49-68.

Jenson, Victoria. 2011. *Charity Faith: A Novel.* Amazon Digital Services.

Johnston, Jamie Christensen (Producer and Director). 2008. *Forgotten Coast* DVD. U.S.: Forgotten Coast Films.

Katrina: South Mississippi Story DVD. 2005. Biloxi: WLOX TV-13.

Kenyon International Emergency Services. 2006. *Hurricane Katrina Response Hurricane Katrina Causes Destruction and Large Loss of Life.* Accessed January 10, 2006 kenyon@kenyoninternational. com

Kirk-Duggan, Cheryl. A. 2006. *The Sky is Crying: Race, Class and Natural Disasters.* Nashville: Abingdon Press.

Knabb, Richard, Jamie Rhome, and Daniel Brown. 2005. *Tropical Cyclone Report: Hurricane Katrina.* National Hurricane Center, National Oceanic Atmosphere Association Accessed January 15, 2006 http://www.nhc.noaa.gov/pdf/TCR-AL122005_Katrina.pdf

Koch, Kathleen. 2010. *Rising From Katrina: How My Mississippi Hometown Lost It All and Found What Mattered.* Wilson: John F. Blair.

Kottak, Conrad. 2006. *Mirror for Humanity* NY: McGraw-Hill.

Laditka, Sarah, Louise Murray, and James Laditka. 2010. In the Eye of the Storm: Resilience and Vulnerability Among African American Women in the Wake of Hurricane Katrina. *Health Care for Women International*, 31:11, 1013-1027.

Landry, Bart. 2002. *Black Women Wives: Pioneers of the America Family Revolution.* Oakland: University of California Press.

Landry, Bart. 1987. *The New Black Middle Class.* Oakland: University of California Press.

Leach, Monica T., Pamela P Martin, Tuere A. Bowles, and Jocelyn D. Taliaferro. 2008. *Our Souls Look Back in Wonder: The Spirituality of African American Families Surviving Hurricane Katrina.* In Dorothy Singleton (Ed) The Aftermath of Hurricane Katrina: Educating Traumatized Children Pre-Kindergarten Through College. University Press of America. 47-62.

Leik, Robert K. Shelia A. Leik, Knutt Ekker, and Gregory A. Gifford. 1982. *Under the Threat of Mount St. Helens, A Study of Chronic Family Stress* as cited in Elaine Enarson and Betty Morrow (Eds) The Gendered Terrain of Disaster: Through Women's Eyes. Minneapolis: University of Minnesota.

Lemert, Charles and Eshe Bham. 1998. *The Voice of Anna Julia Cooper: Including a Voice From the South and Other Important Essays, Papers, and Letters.* NY: Rowman & Littlefield Publishers.

Leonard, Devin. 2005. The Only Lifeline was the Walmart. *Fortune Magazine*, October 3. Accessed November 12, 2005, https://archive.fortune.com/magazines/fortune/fortune_archive/2005/10/03/8356743/index.htm

Litt, Jacquelyn. 2006. Getting Out or Staying Put: An African American Women's Network in Evacuation from Katrina. *National Women's Studies Association Journal* 20: 3, 32-48.

Liu, Amy, Roland Anglin, Richard Mizelle, and Allison Peyer. 2011. *Resilience and Opportunity: Lessons from the U.S. Gulf Coast After Katrina and Rita*. Washington: Brookings Institute.

Levitt, Jeremy I. and Matthew C. Whitaker. 2009. *Hurricane Katrina: America's Unnatural Disaster (Justice and Social Inquiry)*. Lincoln: University of Nebraska Press.

Logue, James N., Holger Hansen, and Elmer Struening. 1979. Emotional and Physical Distress Following Hurricane Agnes in the Wyoming Valley of Pennsylvania. *Public Health Reports* 94: 6 495-502 as cited in Elaine Enarson and Betty Morrow (Eds) The Gendered Terrain of Disaster Through Women's Eyes. Westport: Greenwood Press.

Lofland, John., & Lyn Lofland. 1984. *Analyzing Social Settings*. Belmont: Wadsworth.

Lovell, Anne M. 2014. *Embodied Histories and Charitable Populism in the PostDisaster Controversy over a Public Hospital*. In Hurricane Katrina in Transatlantic Perspective Romain Huret and Randy J. Sparks (Eds). New Orleans: LSU Press.

Luft, Rachel and Shana Griffin. 2008. *A Status Report on Housing in New Orleans after Katrina: An Intersectional Analysis.* Beth Willinger (Eds), Katrina and the Women of New Orleans. Accessed January 10, 2009 http//Tulane.edu/nccrow/upload/ NCCROWreport08-preface/pdf

Lupton, Deborah. 1999. *Discourse Analysis. In Handbook for Research Methods in Health Sciences,* Melbourne: Addison Wesley Longman, Victor Minichiello, Gerard Sullivan, Ken Greenwood, and Rita Axford (Eds) as cited in Sally C. Hunter, Analysing and Representing Narrative Data: The Long and Winding Road January 2010 1:2, Embracing Multiple Dimension.

Manning Marable and Kristen Clarke. 2007. *Seeking Higher Ground: The Hurricane Katrina Crisis, Race, and Public Policy Reader.* NY: Palgrave Macmillan.

Mason, Beverly J. 2012. *Twice removed: New Orleans Garifuna in the Wake of Hurricane Katrina.* In Lynn Weber and Lori Peek (Eds), Displaced Life in the Katrina Diaspora. Austin: University of Texas Press, 83-197.

Mathews, Ricky, Kat Bergeron, and John Fitzhugh. 2005. *Katrina: Eight Hours That Changed the Mississippi Coast Forever.* Gulfport: Sun Herald.

McCarthy, Kevin and Mark Hanson. 2007. *Post-Katrina Recovery of the Housing Market Along the Mississippi Gulf Coast.* Technical Report of the Gulf States Policy Institute. Santa Monica: RAND Corporation.

McDonnell, S., R.P. Troiano, N. Barker, E. Noji, W.G. Hlady and R. Hopkins. 1995. *Evaluation of Long-term Community Recovery from Hurricane Andrew: Sources of Assistance Received by Population Sub-groups.* Disasters 19: 4, 338–47 as cited in Fothergill, Maestas, and Darlington, Race, Ethnicity and Disasters in the United States: A Review of the Literature, Disasters,1999, 23:2, 156-173.

Medlin, Jeffrey, Ray Ball, and Gary Beele. 2005. *Extremely Powerful Hurricane Katrina Leaves a Historic Mark on the Northern Gulf Coast. A Killer Hurricane Our Country Will Never Forget.* Accessed January 10, 2006 http://www.srh.noaa.gov/mob/?n=katrina

Merton, Robert. 1970. Foreword. In Allen H. Barton *Communities in Disaster: A Sociological Analysis of Collective Stress Situation.* NY: Doubleday.

Merton, Robert and Robert Nisbet. 1976. *Contemporary Social Problems.* NY: Harcourt, Brace and World.

Miles & Huberman. 1994. *Qualitative Data Analysis* 2nd edition. Thousand Oaks: Sage.

Mileti, D.S., T.E. Drabek, and J.E. Haas. 1975. *Human Systems in Extreme Environments: A Sociological Perspective.* Boulder: Institute of Behavioral Science, University of Colorado.

Miller, Judith A., Joseph G.Turner, and Edith Kimball. 1981. *Big Thompson Flood Victims: One Year Later* Family Relations 30 (1): 111-116 as cited in Enarson and Morrow (Eds) The Gendered Terrain of Disaster: Through Women's Eyes. Westport: Greenwood Press.

Mitchell, Justin. 2016. When Shops and Eateries Opened Days After Katrina, The Coast. Rejoiced. *The Sun Herald Newspaper*, accessed January 12, 2017 https://www.sunherald.com/news/weather/hurricane/article98373652.html#storylink=cpy

Mittell, Jason. 2017. *Narrative Theory and Adaptation*. NY: Bloomsbury.

Montana-Leblanc, Phyllis. 2008. *Not Just the Levees Broke: My Story During and After Hurricane Katrina*. NY: Atria Books.

Morgan, Curtis. 2013. Hurricane Sandy Ranked as Second-Costliest Storm Behind Katrina. *The Miami Herald* Accessed January 25, 2014 http://www.morrisdailyherald.com/2013/02/13/sandy-ranked-as-second-costliest-hurricane-behind-katrina/aaicvr0/

Moore Harry E. and H. J. Friedsam. 1959. Reported Emotional Stress Following a Disaster. *Social Forces*, 38: 2, 135-139.

Morrow, Betty Hearn, and Brenda Phillips. 1999. What's Gender Got to Do With It? *International Journal of Mass Emergencies and Disasters*, 17:1 5-14.

Morrison, Toni. 2017. *Keynote Address Princeton Slavery Symposium*. Princeton University Lecture. Accessed July, 27, 2018 https://www.facebook.com/PrincetonU/videos/watch-as-nobel-laureate-toni-morrison-delivers-the-keynote-address-at-the-prince/10155990385075774/

Moustakas, Clark. 1994. *Phenomenological Research Methods*. Thousand Oaks: Sage.

Murakami-Ramalho, Elizabeth, and Beth A. Durodoye. 2008. Looking Back to Move Forward: Katrina's Black Women Survivors Speak. *National Women's Studies Association Journal* 20: 3, 115-137.

Nader, Kathleen. 1997. *Treating Traumatic Grief in Systems*. In C. R. Figley, E. Bride, and N. Mazza (Eds) Death and Trauma: The Traumatology of Grieving,. London: Taylor and Francis, 159-192.

Neilsen, Joyce McCarl. 1984. *Sex and Gender in Disaster Research* as cited in Elaine Enarson and Betty Morrow (Eds). The Gendered Terrain of Disaster: Through Women's Eyes. Westport: Greenwood Press.

Neumayer, Eric and Thomas Plumper. 2007. *The Gendered Nature of Natural Disasters: The Impact of Catastrophic Events on the Gender Gap in Life Expectancy, 1981-2002.* Annals of Association of American Geographers, 97:3, 551-566.

Noel, Gloria. 1998. *The Role of Women in Health Related Aspects of Emergency Management: A Caribbean Perspective.* In Elaine Enarson and Betty Hearn Morrow (Eds), The Gendered Terrain of Disasters: Through Women's Eyes. Westport: Greenwood Press 213-224.

Obama, Michelle. 2018. *Becoming.* NY: Crown Publishing.

Ogunyemi, Chikwenye Okonjo. 1985. Womanism: The Dynamics of the Contemporary Black Female Novel in English. *Signs* 11:1, 63-80.

Ohr O'Keefe Museum of Art and Biloxi Visitors Center. 2015. *Katrina +10: You've Seenthe Storm - Now See the Recovery*. Biloxi, Mississippi. Accessed January 10, 2016 https://biloxi.ms.us/katrina-10-opens-to-public-friday-morning/

Oliver-Smith, Anthony. 1996. Annual Review of Anthropology. *Anthropological Research on Hazards and Disasters* 25, 303-328.

Pardee, Jessica Warner. 2014. *Surviving Katrina: The Experiences of Low-Income African American Women*. Boulder: Lynne Rienner Publishers.

Pattillo-McCoy, Mary. 2000. B*lack Picket Fences: Privilege and Peril Among the Black Middle Class*. Chicago: University of Chicago Press.

Patel, Ushma. 2012. *Hurricane Katrina Survivors Struggle with Mental Health Years Later, Study Says*. Accessed January 20, 2013 https://www.princeton.edu/news/2012/01/24/hurricane-katrina-survivors-struggle-mental-health-years-later-study-says.

Patton, Michael Quinn. 2002. *Qualitative Research and Evaluation Methods*. Thousand Oaks: Sage.

Payne, Charles. 1995. *I've Got the Light of Freedom: The Organizing Tradition and Mississippi Freedom Struggle*. Berkeley: University of California Press.

Peacock, Walter, Betty Hearn Morrow, Hugh Gladwin. 1997. *Hurricane Andrew: Ethnicity, Gender, and the Sociology of Disasters*. London: Routledge.

Penner, D'Ann and Keith C. Ferdinand. 2009. *Overcoming Katrina African-American Voices.* NY: Palgrave Macmillan.

Perry, Ronald and Mushkatel. 1986. *Minority Citizens in Disasters.* Athens: University of Georgia Press.

Perry, Ronald and Mushkatel. 2008. *Minority Citizens in Disasters,* Second Edition. Athens: University of Georgia Press.

Petry, Ann. 1947. *A Country Place.* Boston: Houghton Mifflin.

Petry, Elisabeth. 2009. *At Home Insider: A Daughter's Tribute to Ann Petry.* Jackson: University of Mississippi Press.

Phillips, Brenda, 1993. Cultural Diversity in Disasters: Sheltering, Housing, and Long Term Recovery. *International Journal of Mass Emergencies and Disasters,* 11:1, 99-110.

Phillips, Brenda. 1997. Qualitative Disaster Research. *International Journal of Mass Emergencies and Disasters* 15:1, 179-195.

Phillips, Brenda. 2003. *Qualitative Methods and Disaster Research.* In Robert Stallings (Ed) Methods of Disaster Research. Philadelphia: Xlibris. 194-211.

Phillips, Brenda. 2006. *Research Applications in the Classroom.* In Havidan Rodriguez, Enrico Quarantelli, and Russell Dynes (Eds) Handbook of Disaster Research. NY: Springer Press, 456-467.

Phillips, Brenda and Betty Morrow. 2008. *Women and Disasters: From Theory to Practice.* Philadelphia: Xlibris. 5-11.

Phillips, Brenda, Pam Jenkins, and Elaine Enarson. 2008. *Violence and Disaster Vulnerability.* In Brenda Phillips, Deborah Thomas, Alice Fothergill, and Lynn Blinn-Pike (Eds) Social Vulnerability to Disasters. Boca Raton: CRC Press, 279-306.

Phillips, Brenda. 2012. *Gendered Disaster Practice and Policy.* In Emmanuel David and Elaine Enarson (Eds)The Women of Katrina: How Gender, Race, and Class Matter in an American Disaster. Nashville: Vanderbilt Press, 233-244.

Phillips, Brenda. 2014. *Qualitative Disaster Research.* NY: Oxford.

Phillips, Layli. 2006. *The Womanist Reader.* NY: Routledge.

Phillips, Layli, 2012. *The Womanist Idea.* NY: Routledge.

Prince. Samuel Henry. 1920. *Catastrophe and Social Change.* NY: Columbia University.

Quarantelli, Enrico. 2006. *Catastrophes are Different from Disasters: Some Implications for Crisis Planning and Management Drawn from Katrina.* Understanding Katrina: Perspectives from the Social Sciences. Social Science Research Consortium, Accessed January 7, 2007, understandingkatrina.ssrc.org/Quarantelli/

Ransby, Barbara. 2006. Katrina, Black Women, and the Deadly Discourse on Black Poverty in America. *Du Bois Review* 3:1, 219-222.

Reed, Betsy. 2006. *Unnatural Disaster: The Nation on Hurricane Katrina.* NY: Nation Books.

Reid, Megan. 2011. *A Disaster on Top of a Disaster: How Gender, Race, and Class Shaped the Housing Experiences of Displaced Hurricane Katrina Survivors.* Austin: University of Texas.

Reid, Megan. 2012. *Mothering after a Disaster: The Experiences of Black Single Mothers Displaced by Hurricane Katrina.* In Emmanuel David and Elaine Enarson (Eds) The Women of Katrina: How Gender, Race, and Class Matter in An American Disaster. Nashville: Vanderbilt Press, 105-117.

Reid, Megan. 2013. Disasters and Social Inequalities. *Sociology Compass,* 7:11, 984–997.

Rhodes, Jean, Christian Chan, Christina Paxson, Cecilia Elena Rouse, Mary Waters, and Elizabeth Fussell. 2010. The Impact of Hurricane Katrina on the Mental and Physical Health of Low-Income Parents in New Orleans. *American Journal of Orthopsychiatry* 802, 233-243.

Rice, Pranee Liamputtong and Douglas Ezzy. 1999. *Qualitative Research Methods: A Health Focus.* South Melbourne (Australia): Oxford Press.

Riessman, Catherine K. 2008. *Narrative Methods for the Human Sciences.* Thousand Oaks: Sage.

Ripley, A. 2008. *The Unthinkable: Who Survives Disasters.* NY: Harmony.

Rivers, J.P.W. 1982. Women Last: An Essay on Sex Discrimination in Disasters. *Disasters* 6: 4, 256-267.

Saegert, Susan. 1989. Unlikely Leaders: Older Black Women Building Community Households. *America Journal of Community Psychology*, 17: 3, 295-316.

Salecker, Gene A. 1996. *Disasters on the Mississippi: The Sultana Explosion, April 27, 1865*. Annapolis: Naval Institute Press.

Samuelson, Kate. 2017. *How Hurricane Irma and Hurricane Andrew Compare*. Accessed December 10, 2017 https://time.com/4933571/hurricane-irma-versus-hurricane-andrew/

Scanlon, Joseph. 1988. Disaster's Little Known Pioneer: Canada's Samuel Henry Prince. *International Journal of Mass Emergencies*, 6: 3, 213-232.

Scanlon, Joseph. 1997. Human Behaviour in Disaster: The Relevance of Gender. *Australian Journal of Emergency Management*, 11: 4, 2-7.

Scanlon, Joseph. 2006. Two Cities, Two Evacuations: Some Thoughts on Moving People Out. In *Understanding Katrina: Perspectives from the Social Sciences*, Accessed January 10, 2007 understandingkatrina.ssrc.org/Scanlon/

Schiff, B., & Cohler, B.J. 2011. *Telling Survival Backwards: Holocaust Survivors Narrate the Past*. As cited in G. Kenyon, P. Clark. & B. de Vries (Eds) Narrative Gerontology: Theory, Research, and Practice 113-135. New York: Springer.

Science Daily, 2015. *Effect of Hurricane Katrina on Mississippi*. Accessed December 21, 2017 at https://www.sciencedaily.com/terms/effect_of_hurricane_katrina_on_mississippi.htm

Sharkley, Patrick. 2007. Survival and Death in New Orleans: An Empirical Look at the Human Impact of Katrina. *Journal of Black Studies*, 37: 4, 482-501.

Shoaf, Kimberley I. and Sareen R. Harvinder. 1998. Injuries as a Result of California Earthquakes in the Past Decade. *Disasters* 22: 3, 218-235.

Singleton, Dorothy. 2008. *The Aftermath of Hurricane Katrina: Educating Traumatized Children Pre-K through College*. Lantham: University Press of America.

Smith, James P. 2012. *Hurricane Katrina: The Mississippi Story*. Jackson: University of Mississippi Press.

Soroptimist International of the Americas. 2008. *Reaching Out to Women When Disaster Strikes*. Retrieved December 3, 2008 http://www.soroptimist.org/whitepapers/wp_disaster.html

Spence, Patric, Kenneth Lachlan, and Donyale Griffin. 2007. Crisis Communication, Race and Natural Disasters. *Journal of Black Studies*, 37: 4, 539-55.

Stack, Carol. 1975. *All Our Kin: Strategies for Survival in a Black Community*. NY: Basic Books.

Strauss, Anselm and Juliet Corbin. 2007. *Basics of Qualitative Research: Techniques and Procedures for Developing Grounded Theory*, Fourth Edition. Thousand Oaks: Sage.

Strauss, Anselm and Juliet Corbin. 1998. *Basics of Qualitative Research: Techniques and Procedures for Developing Grounded Theory*, Second Edition. Thousand Oaks: Sage.

Squires, Gregory and Chester Hartman. 2006. *There is No Such Thing as a Natural Disaster: Race, Class, and Katrina.* NY: Routledge.

Sullivan, Nancy K. 2015. *Katrina Mississippi Voices from Ground Zero.* NY: Triton Press.

Taylor, John and Josh Silver. 2006. *From Poverty to Prosperity: The Critical Role of Financial Institutions.* In C. Hartman and G. D. Squires (Eds) There is No Such Thing as a Natural Disaster: Race, Class, and Hurricane Katrina. NY: Routledge 233-254.

Tierney, Kathleen, Michael Lindell, and Ronald Perry. 2001. *Facing the Unexpected: Disaster Preparedness and Response in the United States.* Washington: John Henry Press.

Tierney, Kathleen J. 1989. *The Social and Community Contexts of Disaster.* In R. M. Gist and B. Lubin (Eds.) Psychosocial Aspects of Disaster, *11-39.* NY: Wiley.

Tobin-Gurley, Jennifer, Lori Peek, and Jennifer Loomis. 2010. Displaced Single Mothers in the Aftermath of Hurricane Katrina: Resource Needs and Resource Acquisition. *International Journal of Mass Emergencies and Disasters* 28: 2, 170-206.

Tobin-Gurley, Jennifer. 2008. *Hurricane Katrina: Displaced Single Mothers, Resource Acquisition, and Downward Mobility.* Master's Thesis, Department of Sociology, Colorado State University.

Townes, Emilie. 1997. *Embracing the Spirit: Womanist Perspectives on Hope, Salvation, and Transformation.* NY: Orbis.
---- 1994. Voices of the Spirit: Womanist Methodologies in the Theological Disciplines.*The Womanist,* 1:1 1-2.
---- 1993. *Womanist Justice, Womanist Hope.* Latvia: Scholars Press.

---- 1989. Roundtable Discussion: Christian Ethics and Theology in Womanist Perspective. *Journal of Feminist Studies in Religion*, 5: 2, 94-97.

Trethewey, Natasha. 2010. *Beyond Katrina: A Meditation on the Mississippi Gulf Coast*. Athens: University of Georgia.

Triplett, Tommy, Mike McNair, Carol Hopson, Rick Horner, Wings or Anglers, and Buford Myrick, (Photographers). *Mississippi Coast Before and After Hurricane Katrina: Plus Five Years Later*. Ocean Springs: Ocean Springs Dist.

Trivedi, Jennifer. 2020. Mississippi After Katrina: Disaster Recovery and Reconstruction on the Gulf Coast. NY: Rowman and Littlefield.

Troutt, David Dante. 2007. *After the Storm: Black Intellectuals Explore the Meaning of Hurricane Katrina*. NY: The New Press.

Tyler, Pamela. 2007. The Post-Katrina, Semiseparate World of Gender Politics. *Journal of American History*, 94, 780–788.

Turner, Ralph, Joanne Nigg, and Denise Heller Paz. 1986. *Waiting for Disaster: Earthquake Watch in California*. Berkeley: University of California Press.

Unger, David J. and Noble Ingram. 2018. Billion-dollar weather: The 10 most expensive US natural disasters. Accessed December 2, 2018, https://www.csmonitor.com/Environment/2013/0627/Billion-dollar-weather-The-10-most-expensive-US-natural-disasters/Drought-and-heat-wave-2012-32.7-billion

U.S. Bureau of the Census. 2006. American Community Survey. Washington, D.C: U. S. Department of Labor. Accessed January 15, 2006.

U.S. Bureau of the Census. 2006. U.S. Department of Labor, Quarterly Census on Employment and Wages. Washington, D.C: U. S. Department of Labor. Accessed January 15, 2007.

U.S. Bureau of the Census, 2005. *Hurricane Data, Demographic Profile of Katrina-Affected Counties.* Washington, D.C: U. S. Department of Labor. Accessed January 15, 2005 http://www. census.gov/Press-Release/www/205/katrina.htm

U.S. Bureau of the Census, 2004. Hurricane Katrina Data. Washington, DC: U.S. Bureau of the Census. Accessed January 10, 2005 http:// www.cencus.gov/Press-Release/ www/2005/katrina.htm

U.S. Department of Commerce. 2006. *Gulf Coast Recovery: 7 Months after the Hurricanes.* Washington, DC: Economics and Statistics Administration. Access December 29, 2006 www.esa.doc.gov/ reports/2008/December2006.pdf

U.S. Department of Labor, Bureau of Labor Statistics. 2015. *Hurricane Katrina: A Look Back at Employment and Unemployment.* Accessed December 15, 2015. https://www.bls.gov/opub/ ted/2015/hurricane-katrina-a-look-back-at-employment-and-unemployment.htm

Vaill, Sarah. 2006. *The Calm in the Storm: Women Leaders in Gulf Coast Recovery.* Women's Funding Network and Ms. Foundation for Women. Accessed January 5, 2007 www.msfoundation.org

Vaz, Kim. 1997. *Oral Narrative Research with Black Women.* Thousand Oaks: Sage.

Waillo, Keith, Karen O'Neill, Jefferey Dowd, and Roland Anglin. 2010. *Katrina's Imprint: Race and Vulnerability in America.* NY: Rutgers.

Walker, Alice. 2006. Coming Apart. In Layli Philips (Ed), *The Womanist Reader*, 3-20. NY: Routledge.
----. 1998. *Anything We Love Can Be Saved: A Writer's Activism.* NY: Ballantine.
----. 1988. *Living by the Word.* NY: Harcourt Brace.
----. 1983. *In Search of Our Mothers' Gardens: Womanist Prose.* San Diego: Harcourt Brace.

Walker, Camron and Alfonzo Walker. 2015. Hurricane Katrina 10th Anniversary DVD.

Waple, Anne. 2005. Hurricane Katrina. *National Oceanic Atmospheric Administration: National Climatic Data Center.* Asheville, NC. Accessed June 4, 2006 http://www.ncdc.noaa.gov/extremeevents/specialreports/Hurricane-Katrina.pdf

Ward, Jesmyn. 2012. *Salvage the Bones.* NY: Bloomsbury.

Weber, Lynne and Peek, Lori. 2012. *Displaced: Life in the Katrina Diaspora.* Austin: University of Texas Press.

Webb, Eugene, Donald T. Campbell, Richard D. Schwartz, and Lee Sechrest. 1999. *Unobtrusive Measures* (Sage Classic Series, 2). Thousand Oaks: Sage.

Weems, Clenora. 1994. *Africana Womanism: Reclaiming Ourselves.* Lambertville: Bedford Press.

Weems, Renita. 1988. Just a Sister Away: A Vision of Women's Relationships in the Bible. West Bloomfield: Walk Worthy Press.

Weissman, Gary. 2016. *The Writer in the Well: On Misreading and Rewriting Literature. (Theory and Interpretation of Narrative Theory)*. Columbus: Ohio State Press.

Whelan, R. K. 2006. *An Old Economy for the 'New' New Orleans? Post Hurricane Katrina Economic Development Efforts*. In C. Harman and G.D. Squires (Eds) There is No Such Thing as a Natural Disaster: Race, Class, and Hurricane Katrina. NY: Routledge 215-231.

White, Debra Gray. 1985. *Ar'n't I A Woman? Female Slaves in the Plantation South*. NY: Norton.

Wilkerson, Kenneth P. and Perry J. Ross. 1970. Citizens Response to Warnings of Hurricane Camille. As cited in Enarson and Morrow (Eds) *The Gendered Terrain of Disaster:Through Women's Eyes*. Westport: Greenwood Publishing.

Williams, Delores S. 2013. *Sisters in the Wilderness: The Challenge of Womanist God-Talk*. NY: Orbis

Williams, Delores. 1993. *Womanist Theology: Black Women's Voices*. In James Cone and Gayraud S. Wilmore (Eds), Black Theology 1980-1992, 266-270. Maryknoll: Orbis.

Williams, Erica, Olga Sorokina, Avis Jones-DeWeever, and Heidi Hartmann. 2006. The Women of New Orleans and the Gulf Coast: Multiple Disadvantages and Key Assets for Recovery Part II. Gender, Race, and Class in the Labor Market Part 2. *Institute for Women's Policy Research. Publication No. 465* Washington DC. Accessed January 5, 2007 http://www.iwpr.org/initiatives/ katrina-the-gulf-coast#sthash.clryIr1N.dpuf

Wilson, Jennifer, Brenda Phillips, and David M Neal. 1996. Women's Vulnerability to Domestic Violence: Organizational Behavior after Disasters. As cited in Enarson and Hearn Morrow (Eds) *The Gendered Terrain of Disaster: Through Women's Eyes*. Westport: Greenwood.

WLOX: ABC 13. 2005. Katrina South Mississippi's Story DVD. Biloxi Mississippi.

WLOX: ABC 13. 2006. Katrina Building South Mississippi One Year Later DVD. Biloxi Mississippi.

CPSIA information can be obtained
at www.ICGtesting.com
Printed in the USA
BVHW031627140921
616732BV00001B/9